THE TOTAL RELATIONSHIP

FOUR STEPS TO BREAKING THE MOLD,
TRANSFORMING THE CLIENT-FINANCIAL
ADVISOR RELATIONSHIP,
AND BUILDING TRUE WEALTH

TYSON JON RAY

OTHER BOOKS BY TYSON RAY

Your World Impact

THE TOTAL RELATIONSHIP

FOUR STEPS TO BREAKING THE MOLD,
TRANSFORMING THE CLIENT-FINANCIAL
ADVISOR RELATIONSHIP,
AND BUILDING TRUE WEALTH

TYSON JON RAY

ethos
collective

THE TOTAL RELATIONSHIP
Copyright 2023 Tyson Jon Ray
www.FormWealth.com

Published by Ethos Collective
Powell, Ohio
www.EthosCollective.vip

Library of Congress Cataloging: 2023906438
ISBN Hardcover: 978-1-63680-159-9
ISBN Paperback: 978-1-63680-158-2
ISBN E-book: 978-1-63680-160-5

Investments & Wealth Institute™ (The Institute) is the owner of the certification marks "CIMA" and "Certified Investment Management Analyst." Use of CIMA and/or Certified Investment Management Analyst signifies that the user has successfully completed The Institute's initial and ongoing credentialing requirements for investment management professionals.

The Forbes Top Wealth Advisors Best-In-State 2023 ranking, developed by SHOOK Research, is based on an algorithm of qualitative criteria, mostly gained through telephone and in-person due diligence interviews, and quantitative data. This ranking is based upon the period from 6/30/2021 to 6/30/2022 and was released on 4/4/2023. Those advisors that are considered have a minimum of seven years of experience, and the algorithm weights factors like revenue trends, assets under management, compliance records, industry experience and those that encompass best practices in their practices and approach to working with clients. Portfolio performance is not a criteria due to varying client objectives and lack of audited data. Out of approximately 39,007 nominations, 7,321 advisors received the award. This ranking is not indicative of an advisor's future performance, is not an endorsement, and may not be representative of individual clients' experience. Neither Raymond James nor any of its Financial Advisors or RIA firms pay a fee in exchange for this award/rating. Raymond James is not affiliated with Forbes or SHOOK® Research, LLC. Please visit https://www.forbes.com/best-in-state-wealth-advisors for more info.

Source: Barron's "Top 1,200 Financial Advisors," March 2022. Barron's is a registered trademark of Dow Jones & Company, L.P. All rights reserved. The rankings are based on data provided by 6,186 individual advisors and their firms and include qualitative and quantitative criteria. Time period upon which the rating is based is from 09/30/2020 to 09/30/2021, and was released on 03/11/2022. Factors included in the rankings: assets under management, revenue produced for the firm, regulatory record, quality of practice and philanthropic work. Investment performance is not

This material was written with technical assistance from Igniting Souls Publishing.

TABLE OF CONTENTS

INTRODUCTION TO THE TOTAL RELATIONSHIP

There is a reason only 35% of Americans work with a financial advisor.[1] The beliefs and practices of so many advisors are antiquated and wrong. I have dedicated my entire professional career to wealth advising, and I've come to the conclusion my industry needs to shift the focus from money to people, products to plans, and market predictions based on historical data and what is not known about the future results of the markets, economy, and investment rates of return to what is known. This simple redirection allows advisors to concentrate on creating a better life for the client by working in Total Relationship.

This book is my attempt to change what a Financial Advisor can offer a client through what I call The Total Relationship.

The Total Relationship helps the client as well as the advisor understand their roles as they come together to create a mutually beneficial partnership where both lives can become better together.

A great Total Relationship requires a client who wants advice from a professional as well as a professional who knows how to give intelligent suggestions and can lead the client through life. This philosophy offers mutually beneficial incentives to keep the advisor and client together as they live out life, hopefully for the better.

Client's lives are at stake, and each person is worthy of being saved from a product-focused industry.

WHO AM I TO WRITE THIS BOOK

The twenty-year bull market of the 1980s and 1990s laid the foundation for my career and formed my initial perspective. Sadly, a large portion of the financial industry and many individual investors remain focused on facts and feelings from that era. Driven by fear and greed, the client gets the short end of the stick.

To prove my point, watch any movie about the finance industry based on real or fictional characters. The 1987 hit *Wall Street* remained a recruiting tool for banks and firms for thirty years after its release. Subsequently more Hollywood stories offered a skewed portrayal of the worst of the finance industry, sending a variety of negative messages to the world–from the attraction of greed to the fueling of corporate spending and ambition. Unfortunately, these movies and some of the realities they represent have contributed to the fluctuation in the financial industry's reputation I've experienced over the past three decades.

At the end of the twentieth century, the market soared. While many saw significant increases in their portfolios, almost as many experienced exploitation and felt like investment firms had hung them out to dry. Many firms made recommendations on what to buy and sell to individuals based on investments that would benefit the firms more than the clients. Professional investors use the buy low and sell high strategy; however, for this to work, someone else, the unknowing individual investor, must buy high and sell low. This happens even to this day.

My first day in an investment firm revealed that my title of stockbroker would change to financial consultant then financial advisor, yet I felt I needed to be a salesman in order to fulfill the expectation of my employer. Though not at all what I had envisioned, I was instructed to cold-call a lengthy list of potential clients to convince them to invest in the latest promise—the late '90s tech growth stocks or an alternative high-dividend-paying utility.

I called 3,000 people three times in six months, held sixteen different speaking events, and was the hardest working, most unsuccessful salesman in our Pensacola Office. What started as a dream to be successful quickly turned into just trying to survive. I felt stressed trying to meet targets and earn enough commission to buy food. Within six months, I'd moved from salary plus commission to straight commission, and couldn't meet the goals I'd set for myself. In November 1998, my $400 paycheck didn't cover my rent, let alone my car payment or credit card minimum. So, I did what most young people in that position do: I applied for a second credit card so I could pay my bills.

Money symbolized comfort, but it seemed so far out of reach. I worked twelve hours a day, six days a week with little to show for it. A flattened rummage sale bean bag served as my only chair, and my college television sat on the floor in one corner of my tiny apartment. A throwaway piece of counter sprawled over two broken filing cabinets I pulled out of the dumpster created a makeshift desk in the other corner, but without the funds to buy a chair, it wasn't extremely useful. If you had walked in, you'd have assumed someone robbed me.

The only sign that someone might plan on living there for any length of time were the few pictures hanging on the walls—pictures that felt like a metaphor for my life. They represented the face of contentment and cheer I painted on every day as I went to work. I hoped the pictures as well as my smiles would distract me from what hovered underneath, a barely surviving mess. The realization forced me to come to terms with my situation and ask myself, "What am I going to do to change this?"

The Will Smith movie *Pursuit of Happyness* reflected well what my life felt like; except I didn't have a son, and only credit cards kept me from living on the street, but broke and struggling I understood well.

I knew there had to be more to this life. I decided it was time to figure out how to do this job in a way that allowed me to live with myself. Peddling products to reach goals and garner bonuses would never be fulfilling. I didn't want to spend my career trying to convince clients to buy products and services that wouldn't improve their future. In hindsight, I realize I couldn't succeed in sales because I didn't believe I was adding value. I was just doing what everyone else was trying to do, sell stocks to anyone who wanted to buy them.

This Total Relationship Formula was born out of the frustration I experienced my first few months in Pensacola. After graduating from the University of Western Florida, I worked in the industry in that area. It didn't take long for me to realize I wasn't in the place where I could be my best.

An e-mail from my grandmother who lived alone in a little farmhouse in the Midwest gave me the push I needed to move. I had spent countless summers on that small farm. It had offered a young boy comfort and fun during a time when life was hard. So, when Grandma began to struggle living on her own and the email went out to the family saying someone needed to move in or Grandma would need to go into assisted living, I knew what I needed to do.

No one realized my outlook wasn't good, especially my estranged family. I left for college with a plan—I would become successful and never look back. Now I was failing fast. Moving home meant living to survive another day. My family was shocked when I offered to help make sure Grandma got her insulin shots in the morning and be there at night if something happened. For me, it was free living and the opportunity to begin a new chapter in my career.

Just a few days after making arrangements with my grandmother, I walked into the office of the branch manager who had reluctantly hired me and admitted to him he'd been right. No one wanted to trust a guy right out of college with their money.

Moving back to Wisconsin was the perfect decision for me. In addition to being able to care for someone I loved deeply, it offered me the opportunity to step back and reevaluate my life. I left Florida determined to find a niche in the industry. I wanted to make a positive difference in the lives of real people. And that's what I've been doing for the past twenty-five years—learning how to build the Total Relationship with clients.

Thankfully, the firm I left in Pensacola, had a location one town over from Grandma's farm. Before moving back, I got permission to work out of that office. Returning to the area I grew up in would provide a bigger network of prospective clients. The Wisconsin office was nothing compared to Pensacola. I went from working with thirty powerful personalities in an office lined with dark cherry and steeped in old money to an office with two advisors and laminated furniture.

William Decani, the senior office advisor, was a classic stockbroker. In his mid-sixties, he loved the bull market of the 1980s and 1990s. What William didn't like was the industry's growing demand to use technology to do daily business. William used a desk phone and the *Wall Street Journal* for his entire forty-year career. Thus, when I offered to help him with the technology, William seemed to take me under his wing.

My new mentor didn't need me to sell stocks, he was good at that. However, the office had just joined the world of email, and online discount brokers had started their advertising. The new competition would do a stock trade for eight dollars as opposed to a few hundred. Mr. Decani told me the business would never be the same.

So, I had little to do. I had come to terms with my aversion to cold-calling. I wouldn't want someone to do that to me.

In less than a month, I considered changing my career. I walked into William's office and asked to see how much his portfolio was worth. I explained my conundrum. If I was going to stick with this career, I wanted to see the potential. How much could I make over forty years?

William started rummaging around this huge pile of paper on this desk. The foot-high stack often had pens, sticky notes, and reports sliding off the top. It looked like a mess to me, but it was William's mess, and he loved it. He checked a few spots in the pile, pulled out three statements, and after looking them over, he handed them to me.

The statements were a previous month's report for William's IRA, his wife's IRA, and their joint account. Their joint account was worth over a million dollars as were both of their IRAs. I looked up from my quick review to find William staring across his mound of paper waiting for my response.

Many thoughts rushed through my brain. *Wow. that is a lot of money! He made all this gain with just a few stocks in his accounts.*

But what I said next was pivotal in my career, "William, why is your joint account not in a trust?"

William's face transformed from proud to puzzled, "Why would I want my joint account in a trust?"

I allowed a long pause, then carefully asked another question, "Do you know without a trust and some good estate planning your estate may pay over $1,000,000 in taxes when you and Rita both pass?"

William thought for a time then asked the question that would change my future, "Do you know anything about trusts or how to reduce that estate tax?"

At that time, I knew nothing about trusts specifically, but I had read about this estate tax issue in a firm-published brochure. By that time in my career, I had read every piece of literature that our firm's marketing department created—every single one. Why? Because I am a student/teacher. I love to learn and then teach others what I garner. I also am a quick study, and I realized that reading the brochures created for clients helped me learn more quickly and allowed me to go back and dig deeper as needed. These brochures were like the cliff notes of a book.

My inactivity in the arena of cold-calling prospects to sell stocks had given me an opportunity to learn about other products and services. One brochure entitled "Avoiding Estate Taxes" dealt with using trusts for people who were subject to the 50% estate tax, which in 1999 was anyone with accounts over $1,200,000.

Before I could answer William, he had resumed digging around in the pile. He soon pulled out a copy of a check and handed it to me as he explained that a wealthy client had died recently. I still have the copy of that million-dollar check made out to the United States Treasury with the memo stating "1999 Estate Tax." The family had to sell most of their stock holdings to pay the taxes. Avoiding Estate Taxes had quickly become a sensitive subject.

I asked William to give me access to his account so I could run an estate planning illustration and show him how to avoid the estate taxes. He agreed, and off I went to my office. Finally, I had something to do that didn't involve trying to sell stocks.

Given I knew nothing, I decided to get professional help. I called the home office estate planning department and talked to Barb. She turned out to be one of my angels. I honestly explained my dilemma and told her that everything I knew about estate planning, I had read in the firm's brochure. She laughed said, "My job is to teach you what you need to know."

Together Barb and I put together an estate plan to help William and Rita avoid estate taxes. We included trusts, powers of attorney, a charitable trust, and an irrevocable life insurance policy. Barb walked me through the whole process, and after several months, we had a solution for

William and Rita's estate tax problem. William was so grateful for my help in solving his million-dollar problem, he allowed me to keep 100% of the commission of the life insurance policy they purchased.

One year earlier I had earned $400 for the month and thought I had no future in the finance industry. Rather than giving up, I found a way to reduce my expenses and did everything I could to stop selling products and start solving problems—completely counter to the way every advisor I knew worked and backwards from all I had been trained to do.

Less than six months after we put the plan together, I was thrilled to find out my paycheck for that two-million-dollar Second to Die Whole Life Insurance Policy was $40,000—not for the year, but for the month of March 1999. Those funds allowed me to pay off my credit card debts, student loans, and my car. One check set me free. More to the point, William felt good about giving me that premium. It is standard practice for advisors who take life insurance out on themselves to get the commission. In fact, our arrangement was so unheard of that the home office called to make sure the commission going under my rep code wasn't a mistake. William valued the solution I provided and the work I did to help him and Rita; he wanted me to have it.

Clients never mind paying for value. I am reminded of that every time I stand and wait at Starbucks for a five-dollar cup of coffee when the diner next door gives coffee away. Advisors would do better for themselves, and their clients would have better lives, if they focused more on creating value and solving problems than selling a product or portfolio.

Even better than that paycheck, William and I agreed to enter a partnership. I would take his clients through the same estate planning process Barb taught me. Barb and the professionals in the estate planning department would help me make a difference in those clients' lives.

During the next twelve months, I became knowledgeable in estate planning through the wisdom that comes from doing the work of solving problems. At the same time, William's business doubled in size. William took care of the stocks, and I helped clients with the estate planning and allocating the rest of their assets. Our combined revenue exceeded a million dollars during that time. William was named as one of his firm's top producers.

Back then the payout was 50%, so William's compensation was about $400,000 and mine about $100,000 from the life insurance work I had done for the estate planning. My work had brought in $50,000,000 in new assets. Funny thing about those assets was William's frustration because almost none of those assets went into his favorite investment—stocks.

March 2000 gave us the Tech Bubble Peak. Over the next three years, the value of William's beloved stocks dropped by half. Our diversified assets allocations did much better but were still down.

On their fiftieth wedding anniversary trip to Mexico, Rita had a massive heart attack and passed. William lost both his love for picking stocks and the love of his life. At the age of 72, he retired and allowed me to take over his life's work. The agreement came with one stipulation—I would always have a bowl of tootsie rolls or other small candy in the reception area. If you stop in, be sure to take one in honor of William.

I learned in hindsight that not needing the sale always freed me to do what was right. Throwing new advisors into the career field and neglecting to provide them with the assets to do well can be detrimental to everyone. Without the ability to earn a living wage, it becomes tempting to take shortcuts or focus on short-term profits instead of long-term relationships. William helped me get on my feet and begin to develop the strategy I now use to help clients. The trust he placed in me allowed me to find a space that wasn't merely profit-centered but happiness and quality of life focused.

I started this venture as a newly married twenty-seven-year-old. For the first time since graduation, I finally was in the driver's seat. I didn't aim for sales; I didn't have quotas. The quantity of new clients didn't matter. I had the resources to take time and build genuine relationships. I knew that I'd just skimmed the surface of this vital industry-success strategy, and I felt thrilled to consider what the future held.

Now I am better able to understand better the importance of the dynamic between a financial advisor and client. The Total Relationship allows me to make our joint effort as prosperous and fulfilling as possible. I hope by sharing my strategies with you, we can reshape the industry for the better by breaking the mold of old mindsets, transforming our partnerships, and building true, lasting, and fulfilling wealth.

SECTION ONE:

BREAKING MOLDS

People use molds with the expectation of reproducing the outcome. It didn't take long for me to see this was a problem with the traditional mold of stockbroker even after the industry retitled it financial advisor.

After William retired, I rethought our methods of serving clients and decided to get out of individual stocks. We had just experienced the longest and deepest market decline in decades. Several companies had declared bankruptcy, and I never again wanted to call clients to tell them about their individual stock investments becoming worthless.

Another reason I wanted out of stocks stemmed from clients' responses in the fall of 1999 and spring of 2000. I advised many to get out of their stock positions—taking a profit or hedging their losses. Responses ranged from not wanting to pay my commission or the capital gains tax to holding on until the stock recovered. 'Buy low and sell high' is almost impossible when you have to get a client's approval to make the decision. Of course, after the market decline, they all wished they would have taken my suggestion.

The lesson I learned was that clients' behaviors are their greatest risk to their own investments. About that same time, I came across two different research studies that provided the guidance I needed to break free.

THE DALBAR STUDY

DALBAR Incorporated's "Quantitative Analysis of Investor Behavior" used returns from 1986 through 2005 to report that the average investor had a 3.7% annualized return compared to the market return of 13.2%. Let that sink in because that is not a typo; the average investor underperformed the market by more than half the return available. Since 1994, DALBAR has shown that the average investor seldom remains in an investment long enough to achieve the average return. Annually there is proof the average investor underperforms their own investments.

Since 1984, approximately 70% of average investor underperformance occurred during only ten key periods of market crises. Of the ten most severe cases of underperformance, eight would have produced better returns for the average investor one year later if he or she had held on to those investments. [2]

These statistics helped me see I could make life better for clients by not allowing them to decide when to buy and sell their investments. Additionally, it would break the mold of merely investing all their money and focusing on what money should be invested. It became important to me to give professional advice on the funds clients held outside of their investments, allowing me to help the average client so they could see investment returns that were close to the returns of the market.

AMERICAN FUNDS STUDY

The second study, done by American Funds, reported the best-selling funds by sector compared to the best performing ones.

Year	Top Selling Fund Type	Top Performing Fund Type
1990	Large Cap Stock Funds	Money Market Funds
1991	Money Market Funds	Small Cap Stock Funds
1992	Small Cap Stock Funds	International Stocks
1993	International Stocks	High Yield Bond Funds
1994	High Yield Bond Funds	Money Market Funds
1995	Money Market Funds	Small Cap Stock Funds
1996	Small Cap Stock Funds	Large Cap Stock Funds
1997	Large Cap Stock Funds	Large Cap Stock Funds

Do you see the pattern? Each year, advisors sold and investors bought funds based on what did well the year before, only to find that another fund performed better. Then in 1997 they got it right – Large Cap Stocks were both the top selling and top performing. This trend continued for the next three years and was very successful—until it wasn't. The market decline in 2000 and 2001 wiped out most of the over performance taking them back to 1997 levels. This is textbook buying high with hopes it will go higher. It often does not pan out well for the investor and is a prime example of the financial services industry's long history of selling based on past performance.

Every industry has old "molds" that worked in the past. These molds feel good because they have done well in the past, and no one appreciates feeling good more than financial services clients. So, the industry has created tons of these investments based on what has done well recently. Financial advisors end up charging a fee for the equivalent of last week's winning lotto numbers.

The biggest reason advisors stick with past performance (old molds) is because a *known* strategy feels better than an *unknown* strategy. Fear holds the industry hostage. No one wants to venture into unfamiliar territory. But it took brave souls to be pioneers in the wild west.

Like molds in the ceramic and steel industry, financial models need to be replaced every decade or so. Old molds in those tangible product industries cause cracks and imperfections in dishware and train parts; similarly, they create fragmented relationships and destroy trust in the financial realm. Our molds are like everything else in the world; as new information and experience become available, updates need to take place. Consider how businesses would be hindered if they still relied solely on landlines now that cell phones are the norm. And stores that rely on manual cash registers that don't offer end of day reports nor tell employees how to make change are considered old-fashioned. In the same way, thinking that the financial molds of the seventies continue to perform adequately would be ignorant and only serves to foster more broken relationships.

Breaking molds and moving from the known to the unknown can be scary, but learning how to synthesize everything we've learned over time and create new molds can be extremely rewarding.

The Financial Service Industry has been perceived as one of fear and greed. When people think about financial advisors, they think Wall Street and deception used for financial gain. This perception has some validity. My goal is to change the negative view of financial service and reveal its beauty as well as its ability to make people's lives better for generations.

CHAPTER ONE:

COMMON MOLDS THAT NEED BROKEN

BREAKING THE MOLD OF FOMO

FoMO finally made the Oxford Dictionary in 2013 though it's a concept that's been driving humans since the beginning of time. Marketing firms have been using it to their clients' advantage for decades, and it has been the downfall of more than one teenager. It's a descendant of keeping up with the Joneses.

The financial industry isn't exempt from the pitfalls of the Fear of Missing Out. However, this twenty-first century trap begins with another mold: the conversation around performance. Financial advisors, and the industry for that matter, try to define an advisor's value by investment performance. Ironically, the performance of the markets and rates of return are things no one can control. We can control *where* and *when* we expose ourselves to them and when we get out of them, certainly. But what happens while we're in them is like trying to control the wind.

Regardless, investment statements continue to reflect the historical wind patterns. Yes, performance charts allow us to see what is possible. But there is a more important conversation than the performance of accounts.

Clients focused on performance often fall into the mold of FoMO because they feel they should be doing what everyone else is doing. However, the diversity of clients' past and future plans as well as their present ability to invest means that what everyone else is doing often will not be the best approach in terms of investing. As advisors, it can be tempting to fall into this FoMO trap and invest where the masses go, especially if we experience push back from the client.

Total Relationship Advisors turn the conversation from monitoring the portfolio to making sure they understand the person. They focus on helping the client understand how their investments relate to their goals rather than explaining how their portfolio is invested, what the allocation is, and how it's performing relative to its appropriate benchmark.

The performance discussion changes to an evaluation of a life well-lived. Did you take that vacation or buy that car? Did we fund that college education? How is the remodel or addition coming? Did we meet our savings goals and avoid taxes as we planned?

As we check off our accomplishments and identify how we should move forward, we sometimes find hopes, dreams, and wishes have changed. We may cross off past goals and add new ones because now we monitor the truly important.

Our level of performance as financial advisors shouldn't be based on some percentage on a backward-looking chart or statistic. We should base the success of our performance on how well our clients live their lives and whether or not they see improvements. Are they happy and content? Do they have regrets? What can we learn going forward? How can we do things better? My conversations with clients have almost nothing to do with the performance of accounts, sub-accounts, investment strategies, or allocations. I don't hide from those topics; it's just that other conversations add more value to the relationship.

I prefer to focus on the value I bring by giving them permission to go enjoy life with the resources we have created. What is the point of exceptional investment performance if the client never accomplishes their passions and desires?

At the end of the day, we focus on these questions:

1. Why are we working together?
2. What are you trying to accomplish?
3. Why are we trying to do it?

If the client's main goal is to just make more money, then we're not a good fit. That doesn't interest me. I could double or triple my practice if I worked with every client that wanted to make money for the sake of having more money. But those who strive after money are never satisfied. On the flip side, clients who care more about the cash flow available to live life to the fullest and enjoy retirement than the return on investments today, experience joy-filled days with much less anxiety.

I've come to realize that as much as we'd like to think more money would solve all our problems, more money often equals more stress and more worries. On the other hand, more love, joy, peace, and contentment bring a better life. All of that is possible for clients when we manage a portfolio well.

More importantly, in the end, our clients pay us a fee to help them get meaning out of their money. Professionals help clients add or take away from their accounts in ways that will help them avoid regretting the decision the rest of their lives.

One of the most difficult decisions for clients is how and when they allow themselves to take money out of the portfolio and enjoy it. In the end, we find it's not portfolio management that clients ultimately pay us for. Rather, Total Relationship Advisors quickly discover they are in the permission granting business. In the simplest terms, clients delegate the responsibility of how they spend their money. Yes, we manage their portfolios and maintain oversight of their finances. However, being responsible as a fiduciary is more. It means caring for the people who've entrusted us to save them from regrets and watching over the friends and family that these people become.

Falling into the mold of FoMO will only hurt the client in the long run. Moving into the new path of choosing the unknown and not following the masses is one of the first steps toward freeing yourself from the broken relationship. The mold of FoMO is a difficult one to break, but still incredibly necessary and worth the effort.

BREAKING THE MOLD OF APPEASEMENT

The mold of appeasement may be the most difficult mold to break. After all, keeping clients happy is undoubtedly the easiest way to create a façade of a client-advisor relationship. What better way to maintain a client than to let them do whatever they want? The urge to satisfy in the short-term instead of giving clients long-term security will always be one of the most dangerous molds in the industry.

One of the most difficult and important aspects of being an advisor is learning that being in the permissions business also means saying no. When a client asks if they should buy their dream car but it's not time yet, it's easy to say, "Why not? Just this once." But "just once" quickly devolves into "just one more time" until eventually your role as an advisor has become substantially less than it should be.

A trusted advisor in a Total Relationship guides the client and helps them act responsibly. Saying "no, we need to wait" or "yes, you should do this now" will empower clients to live their best life. So, professional advisors need to learn to speak with integrity. Though jokes abound about how much people distrust highly paid professionals, clients and patients will listen to doctors, accountants, and attorneys who still speak with brutal honesty.

Appeasement lets a client think they can enjoy today at the expense of their future and not have regrets. While we have to address the stress that comes from limited resources, a financial advisor has done his or her job well when the client experiences a balance of time and money. While we want them to have enough to live comfortably at retirement, we also don't want them to reach the end of their lives with more money than they need, regretting all they didn't do.

Unfortunately, these scenarios are all too common. Some clients retire too soon. Others don't plan strategically for home or automobile purchases, while even more fund their adult children's mistakes. A financial advisor who cares about their client and refuses to live in this mold of appeasement will protect their clients from themselves, helping them make the sacrifices necessary to enjoy a thirty-plus-year retirement. A recent survey discovered that 51% of Americans making over $100,000 [3] each year live paycheck to paycheck. Continuing that lifestyle after retirement requires two million in assets. But how does somebody living paycheck to paycheck save that much? Sacrifices must be made, and regardless of the pain of the conversation, those sacrifices will be greatly influenced by financial advisors willing to speak boldly with integrity.

I learned the pitfalls of appeasement early in my career. In my first year as a financial advisor, a friend of mine reached out when his dad, Jerry, passed. He hoped I could help his mom, Linda. Jerry had built a tech company that paid Linda two million dollars from two separate locations.

I took my first-ever flight, and donning my best suit and feeling incredibly nervous, I flew to California. I hopped into my rental car, drove through the 18,000 lanes of LA traffic, and after checking into my hotel, headed to Linda's house.

Linda was an incredible woman with a heart of gold. A mother of three, Jerry's wife had a wonderful smile and a ton of wit. All this masked the deep sadness that comes with losing a fully loved spouse. We sat down to dinner and talked about our careers, our aspirations, and good times. I felt honored and grateful to have found some light in this tragedy. Leaving Linda's house, I felt fulfilled and excited to come back the next day and discuss our next steps.

The following morning, I met with Linda and her three kids around the kitchen table. To my surprise, my friend and his oldest sibling stepped up to take charge of the discussion. Jerry had made most of his money in the technology sector, so when we began to discuss where to invest, the family immediately leaned toward one sector: technology. All advisors know that with all the areas available for investing, limiting yourself to one is often not the best course of action. I began to tell them this, but they pushed back. The family thought that since Jerry had made the money in that arena, it made the most sense to keep it there.

Brand new to the industry, and after spending a bit of time explaining the reason I recommended multiple avenues, I decided it was more important to land this rather large account than to make sure the family acted in accordance with my recommendations or to simply walk away. Rather than doing what I knew was right, I agreed to allow the family to invest 75% in the technology sector. They used the other 25% to follow my suggestion to diversify outside of technology. I left that day with two checks for one million dollars each and flew back to O'Hare feeling like the king of the castle. My pride carried me all the way back to Wisconsin.

Back home, I proceeded to invest the funds as agreed and created some follow up tasks to discuss updating Linda's estate plan. All was well until the tech bubble burst in March of 2000. Within six months, their two million was worth less than one million. Panicked, I called Linda and told her that to do damage control, we needed to diversify the portfolio based on risk-adjusted returns as I originally wanted to. She agreed, and we made the change, but the damage had already been done.

The next month, I returned to California to talk with Linda. We walked along the Pacific, kicking up sand until we found a bench overlooking the ocean. We sat, and as the waves licked the beach in front of us, Linda began to cry. She confided that she felt she had squandered Jerry's financial legacy. I comforted her and told her she could still retire as planned. The portfolio was salvageable, but we couldn't undo what had already been done.

Sitting next to Linda on that bench, I decided I wanted to do more than merely appease clients. Her tears and grief could have been saved had I been willing to put my foot down. My appeasement caused more pain after the fact than my no would have created at that first meeting.

How can I make my client's life better if I lose their money by following their lead instead of doing what is right? What a client wants is not always what a client needs, and to be a Total Relationship Advisor, we must be willing to give brutally honest, sage advice and stick to it.

Twenty-five years later, Linda remains a client. We were able to build back most of that wealth, and Linda was able to retire in peace. When we talk, she tells stories of grandkids and good times. Our relationship persevered after our mistakes, but I have never forgotten the tears Linda shed as she regretted a decision she made, and I allowed. I learned the hard way that appeasing clients is the most important mold to break.

Total Relationship Advisors commit to being accountable to their clients' future, and their integrity forces them to hold their clients accountable to their goals, so they can achieve the fullest future they can afford. By keeping accountability and integrity at the forefront of our mission, we can steer clients away from poverty and help them reach the destination they've been looking forward to.

The Total Relationship encompasses everything necessary to build foundational trust, cultivate partnerships, and allow both the client and the advisor to feel fulfilled. People often think being a financial advisor simply means handling money; however, in order to create the best investments and help clients plan for a joy-filled future, it's imperative that we know and understand these people who trust us with their future.

Committing to establishing the Total Relationship won't always be easy. It's tempting to limit our involvement to working with dollars. But this old way of advising leaves both the advisor and the client living at less than the optimal points of success and happiness.

I've spent years dreaming of ways to enhance the client-financial advisor relationship. During those same years, I've gained wisdom through failing and succeeding. Some clients' stories have broken my heart, while others have achieved more than they ever thought possible.

SALESMAN OR ADVISOR?

One of the problems I've seen bring pain to many potential clients is the sales mold. Too many advisors mistakenly take on the role of salesman. Total Relationship Advisors understand that their role is to assist people to have a life that is more than just money. Advisors who realize this help their clients experience the best life possible.

Some advisors begin meetings with a cookie-cutter question and answer session solely to identify how much money is available. Rather than getting to know the client, these advisors begin by looking for the best way to sell a product. Firms across the globe offer incentives that encourage advisors to sell the newest idea, trinket, or theory. Free lunches and trainings on best-selling practices send advisors into the masses to share products with current and future clients.

These enticing perks result in sales modes disguised as advising, and the training convinces firm employees they're giving good counsel when in reality, they are simply peddling the newest trend. Worse still, firms spend billions of dollars in marketing each year with the sole purpose of selling ideas and products rather than actually building wealth.

When I started my career, dot com stocks ruled. Many firms pushed the idea that stock ownership was easy and doable. They boasted that an advisor was not needed any more, and initial public offerings (IPOs) became the hot topic of the industry. The bandwagon of growth stock became so popular that when I met with prospective clients, they brought up the subject before I had the opportunity.

The Total Relationship helps clients realize that what the industry advertises as popular and exciting isn't necessarily what will be fruitful in the future, and convincing clients of this truth involves true trust. Portfolios are like bars of soap, the more you handle them the smaller they get. Teaching clients to move away from a more-money mentality and allow their portfolio to grow is a worthwhile endeavor. The training helps clients better understand the difference between building riches and wealth stewardship.

The financial salesman knows about products, latest trends, and the quest for more money. A trusted advisor understands they need to change the focus to a better life.

When we consider trusted counselors or professionals, we think of doctors, lawyers, or preachers. Our brains don't naturally go to financial advisors. Until I decided to become a CERTIFIED FINANCIAL PLANNER™ (CFP®) I didn't understand why advisors had such a low-scale reputation. I felt I'd always been trustworthy with my clients and for the most part, I saw that same trustworthiness within my coworkers.

My partner Luke had already received his certification, and he inspired me to pursue my own. By the time I resolved to take the training, I was nearly ten years into the business. I had been managing over $100 million in client assets and had weathered the tech bubble with thousands of clients. As a branch manager, an officer, and one of the largest advisors at my firm, I pursued the CFP certification because I could, not because I thought I needed it.

The training was held over several days in a hotel in the suburbs of Northern Illinois. Though I looked forward to the first session on retirement, I felt like I already knew just about everything I needed to on the subject. By lunchtime, I realized I'd been quite wrong. Overwhelmed and shocked by how much I didn't know, I headed back into the sessions a bit humbled.

I decided right then that my ego would not take control of my career. Instead, I would return to being a lifelong student and correct my erroneous thinking.

We need to redefine the definition of expert within the financial industry and potentially within every profession. I believe an expert constantly learns and corrects his thinking as new knowledge arises.

I felt the same way when I became a Certified Investment Management Analyst (CIMA™) a few years later. I found myself yet again put in my place by all I didn't know. I began to question why I had been allowed to manage money without that certification. It felt exhilarating to study so hard for an all or nothing, pass/fail exam. I crammed until all hours of the night to make sure I knew the information like the back of my hand. Because of that diligent work, I have retained that knowledge and applied it many times since.

Total Relationship Advisors recognize that accountability means continually pursuing further education and gaining information when available. Integrity involves passing that information along and explaining it as plainly as possible to clients. Total Relationship Advisors, not salesmen, use everything they learn to strategize with and advocate for their clients.

CHAPTER TWO:

BREAKING THE MOLDS OF PAST PERFORMANCE AND STRIVING FOR MORE

In nearly every scenario in the last chapter, one of the driving factors in those stories was past performance of investments. And while professionals will use long-term past performance as a guide, it's important to understand how using this mold as your main source of decision making can be disastrous.

DON'T USE YESTERDAY'S LOTTERY NUMBERS TO INVEST IN THE FUTURE

No one who plays the lottery would use Tuesday's numbers as a guide for Wednesday's ticket. Even the novice player understands that yesterday's drawing has no effect on today's winners. Fortunately, investing has proven more predictable than the lottery; however, it's not as cut-and-dry as taking last year's numbers and playing them again.

One of the great financial-advising misconceptions is that advisors can simply look at what has done well in the past to project the best way to move forward with portfolios. Commercials boasting past performance and what recently has done well reinforce this mentality. Prospective clients compare what they hear to what their portfolio did and are tempted to, and often do, switch to what worked in the past year in hopes it will boost their portfolios. The smiling faces on the screen imply those past returns will also increase happiness. Total Relationship Advisors have learned not to buy into the promotions of what has done well.

Independent fund analyzers rate funds according to how well they performed in the last twelve months based on various criteria of the fund's successes or failures. The majority of clients, and even a few advisors, find it tempting to invest in four- and five-star funds that clearly had success in the past. At face value, this seems logical; nevertheless, two- and three-star funds almost always outperform better-rated funds over time. Annual performance ratings only provide a record of a fund's performance in the prior year, and short-term ratings cannot predict the future. What goes up, comes down; what has not gone up, eventually does.

Many clients focus on last year's portfolio return. An appeasement-based advisor can be persuaded to ignore long-term numbers. Because past performance always offers the hindsight view, the appeaser will find a better performing portfolio. Unfortunately, as handy and simple as it would be, that method will most often prove devastating for both the advisor and client. Clients end up accepting the best performing portfolio only to buy in high and find out it's no longer the best. Worse, they often end up locked in only to find their portfolio underperforming. Why? Because over time all areas of the market end up falling into average.

Ironically, investing has the potential to look very counterintuitive. If the process was really as simple as looking at last year's numbers and acting, few would need a financial advisor. But current trends aren't necessarily good predictors of what will happen in the future. Often, those funds with the highest short-term rating reveal what *not* to invest in or explore as a future option.

Clients with more than one advisor often will mistakenly use past performance to determine which suggestions to follow, not realizing that without fully researching why that particular investment had positive performance, they may be putting their investments at risk. Without a thorough investigation, they may as well play yesterday's lottery numbers.

Advisors can fall into this trap just as easily. The idea that past successes are indicative of future successes can be an attractive concept. I fell victim to this mentality around the turn of the century when the market looked entirely different than it does today.

Between 1999 and 2000, it seemed as though every investment had tripled in a mere twelve-month period. When the market booms, everyone–other advisors and potential clients–asks one central question: how are your investments performing? Prospective clients want to make sure the portfolios you manage are as successful as the rest of the industry before they trust you with their money management, and other advisors use your success to brag or rate their own success.

During that time, we did very well. The fertile economic climate made it easy to excel. We shared our great success with prospective clients and told them future prospects looked every bit as promising. I enjoyed showing them exactly how my hard work was paying off. The tech boom carried every advisor's choices, including mine.

Aided by the incredibly strong markets, we used our positive performance to demonstrate how well we had done when potential clients asked the inevitable question, "How has your performance been recently?" Clients expressed awe when they saw the fantastic growth in their portfolios, and new clients were quick to trust us.

Despite what we know of economics and market cycles, in the midst of the highs it is easy to forget that what goes up will eventually come down—and sometimes rapidly. When the tech bubble burst, our investments began to crumble. Hundreds of portfolios that had been entrusted to us began to fail. Watching the fallout for average families was painful.

I thought back to those first months of extreme growth. We brought in scores of new clients and had celebrated our tremendous success on the company dime. I was appalled to think we'd fallen for the false promise of short-term wealth that wouldn't waver and taken our clients with us.

We had ignored a basic rule of investing. When looking at past performance, we should be looking at trends over decades, not over a few years. A true depiction of how well a company is able to navigate market trends and build successful investments comes from research and practice, so a long-term projection is imperative. Clients should beware of advisors trying to sell investments based on short-term performance.

Total Relationship Advisors understand that a spreadsheet full of impressive percentages of past performance doesn't yield the cash flow that will equate to a life well-lived for clients in the future. Clients don't need percentages; they need Total Relationship Advisors who help them achieve investment performance that will enable them to fix their furnace, pay for college, or take that well-earned European retirement vacation.

Advisors must build meaningful trust with clients. Using yesterday's lottery numbers—short-term investment history—as a way to build that trust proves weak and as short-lived as the boom. In order to be truly accountable to clients, it is vital that we fully explain the way the market works and help them see the difference between decades of performance and a few years. Using misleading numbers does not exhibit the integrity that Total Relationship Advisors should be striving to achieve.

During my first few years of investing, I found that one of the best ways to convey both accountability and trust was through home visits. Sitting down at their kitchen table shows clients that we care about really getting to know them and demonstrates our willingness to do the work of learning about them.

A MORE PERSONAL APPROACH

Denise held a large portfolio, and her advisor had left for a competing firm. Our firm assigned Denise's account to me. When she took my call, she was considering staying with her advisor and moving her accounts to his new firm. I had been working in the field long enough to know that her current advisor had allowed the relationship to focus on performance, treating past numbers as future facts. During my call, I asked Denise if I could visit her at home. She was surprised I was willing to travel to Florida to meet with her and told me it was not necessary. But I shared that I preferred to meet her face-to-face and booked a plane ticket.

When I arrived, I invited her to dinner. I wanted us to get to know each other a bit. We went to an Outback Steakhouse near her home where Denise told me she only wanted half a baked potato with her dinner. I laughed and told her I would eat the other half. As we enjoyed our steaks and shared a potato, we laughed about how absurd we must have looked, two grown adults sitting in a steakhouse each eating half a baked potato.

The next morning, I returned to her home. She received a phone call as we sipped our morning coffees and made small talk. It was the current advisor calling from his new firm. They had the paperwork ready for her to sign to move her accounts. She glanced my way before saying confidently, "No thank you, goodbye." Our dinner the night before and my presence in her home allowed me to gain an important client that would later become a friend. My willingness to eat dinner with her and spend time talking about life over coffee was more meaningful than hearing about better performance.

Home visits offer one easy way for clients to see the Total Relationship Advisor's integrity and desire to be accountable. There in Denise's living room, I was able to show her the value we place on relationship as well as my passion to help her plan for the future. Without that visit, I wouldn't have been able to explain how numbers can be misleading and how our firm cared fully about making sure she lived life to the fullest. Future accountability and integrity will always be more important than the numbers that struck it big yesterday.

BECOME RECESSION PROOF

In order to avoid using yesterday's statistics as guides to future investing, advisors should also have a full understanding of what a recession is or is not, and the best ways to navigate them. The most common belief holds that a recession is "two consecutive quarterly declines in real Gross Domestic Product."[4] I would disagree.

Instead, I appreciate the National Bureau of Economic Research (NBER) definition. They say that a recession is defined as a "significant decline in economic activity spread across the economy, lasting more than a few months, normally visible in real GDP, real income, employment, industrial production, and wholesale-retail sales."

In the normal ups and downs of the economy and business cycles, a recession begins as the economy starts to decline and ends when the economy begins to grow again. The NBER's Business Cycle Data Committee declares starting and ending dates for recessions. Since they attempt to be definitive, not timely, it may be a year or more (allowing for revisions to the economic data) before they make an official pronouncement.

For instance, during the 2001 recession, I served as a young financial advisor working under a mentor. The NBER announced the recession in November and announced that it was over in March 2003. If we marked the dates of the recession by the announcements, we'd have lived through a two-and-a-half-year recession. However, the actual dates according to the March 2003 declaration were March 2001 until that November.

Recessions are not new; we have had as many as forty-seven recessions in the United States dating back to the Articles of Confederation; however, World War II marked the beginning of major modern economic statistics. Between 1945 and 2001, ten different recessions hit the United States. Each time, the country faced, on average, ten months of decline accompanied by fifty-seven months of expansion. Thus, the population saw about one recession every five years. [5]

The most recently announced United States recession occurred just as I celebrated my forty-fifth birthday. The pandemic of 2020 had ushered in severe economic turmoil. More than 24 million people in the United States lost jobs over a three-week span in April. The official economic impact of the virus has yet to be determined. Despite the lengthy quarantine, job loss, and multiple business closings, the NBER proclaimed only two months of recession–one of the shortest on record. The brief downturn was helped in part by online purchases, zero interest rates, and the Feds attempt to prop up the economy by injecting the largest payouts in history to businesses and individuals. What is interesting is by the time NBER announces a recession has begun, it has usually ended. If you wait on the NBER to announce the fact, it might be too late.

Jack Bogle, the founder of Vanguard, gave this advice to investors: "Don't do something! Stand there!" When it comes to investing, if emotions and common-sense start driving you to do something, don't do it. This can be a difficult concept to grasp, especially when we start talking about accountability. Advisors with integrity feel responsible for their clients' best interests. So, in 2020, when the first few million people lost their jobs, panic set in. As small businesses began to fold, the stress level rose. Holding steady became difficult. But we can't assume a recession is at hand just because headlines predict gloom and doom. It's a mistake to sell market shares when tragedy strikes, or a recession is announced. We run the risk of missing months of recovery and end up buying investments back at higher levels. Recessions are only identifiable with hindsight.

The next recession we enter will be no different than those in the past. Those who allow panic to drive their decisions will most likely regret it. History demonstrates that investing works best when we enter for the long run. Believe it or not, the longer you retain your investments, the lower your chance of losing money and the higher your chance of building significant wealth.

Recessions, just like lottery numbers, are unpredictable, and Total Relationship Advisors understand that. They remain transparent as they admit that no one can predict what will happen during a recession or even when one will occur. Accountability for action as well as inaction is a key part of the Total Relationship. Telling our clients plainly what we can and cannot predict and being honest about what we know and don't know provides a foundation for trust and gives the clients a feeling of security about allowing us to stand guard over their futures.

One strategy we embrace comes from Nick Murray. For over four decades, Nick has correctly encouraged advisors to help their clients see the benefits of owning and overweighting investments in equities. He also addresses the importance of knowing the client's lifestyle and cash flow needs so we can maintain a two-year cash flow reserve. This allows us to avoid selling when the markets are down. Total Relationship Advisors embrace this philosophy because they know this will help clients tolerate the temporary declines that come with recession.

LEAVING BEHIND BUY AND HOLD INVESTING

The number one principle of a Total Relationship Advisor is remembering we are in the people business not the product business. Most clients don't leave because of bad performance, and even if they do, when they discover you had their best interest in mind all the time, they often come back. Still, performance and product-based portfolios often capture the advisor's focus.

Over the years, I've learned and used the principles of those flawed molds from the 1900s. And while some still have an important place in investing, I've discovered places where they can and should be improved and replaced. One mold I'd like to break or recreate is the concept of "buy and hold." This strategy buys shares and holds them regardless of fluctuations in the market. I still employ this long-term investment approach at times. Buy and hold has proven to be profitable–most of the time.

Unfortunately, the average life of a publicly traded company is predicted to drop to less than twenty years in the next decade. [6] At their start, success inflates and allows the business to scale; the company becomes bigger and bigger, bringing growth and gains in market share. Unfortunately, rapid growth makes the enterprise harder to manage internally and suddenly their success becomes their demise.

In the last twenty-five years, I have worked with many clients that purchased a basket of stocks thirty to forty years ago. Most of these clients lived through the Great Depression or fought in World War II. When I showed up at their doorstep to help them prepare their estate or figure out how they will be able to live off their decades-old portfolio of individual stocks, we uncovered problems. Each pool had ten to twenty different holdings, and of those one or two had survived. The others were worthless. These companies had declared bankruptcy, been bought out, or were penny stocks that hadn't grown for decades.

This makes the "buy and hold" model a risky proposition. It needs to be replaced with a long-term solution—a plan and a portfolio created within the advisor-client relationship—one that is managed with discretion based on the client's short-term and long-term needs.

Although the strategy of a Model Portfolio is incredibly well-known in the industry, there is no such thing. The concepts of model portfolios and "buy and hold" investing can be great starting points for understanding the market; however, they won't get us to our goals without the proper planning.

I started working at the age of twelve. With my first paycheck, I opened a Chubby Chipmunk account, created for young first-time account holders. I put all my paychecks into it, learned to save, and received a lot of joy from seeing the meager interest appear over time. However, a Chubby Chipmunk account would not work for my investments today. The idea of a Model Portfolio works in a similar way—as a great starting point.

The Model Portfolio's main flaw is that it begins with the assumption that all clients are the same. Clients come to advisors with a variety of hopes, dreams, aspirations, financial situations, backgrounds, and priorities. Every portfolio needs to be different because every client is different. Using a Model Portfolio opens the conversation with a client, but it has to be greatly altered after we get to know what is important to *the client.*

A huge part of taking a broken relationship to the Total Relationship is recognizing we don't live in a one-size-fits-all world.

THE DIFFERENCE BETWEEN VALUE & WORTH

A key concept to understand when breaking the mold is the fact that many investors think worth and value are the same. We measure worth in dollars. Kelly Blue Book™ attaches a dollar range to used cars. Value, on the other hand, involves an emotional attachment or a long-term relationship. A four-year-old finds value in a second-hand teddy bear because his big brother put it in his cradle. A teen values a rock he stubbed his toe on in the ocean during a family vacation. And a car that KBB priced at $4,000 can be considered priceless to the owner whose deceased grandfather helped him with the body work.

Understanding this principle in relation to big investment purchases like home owning can help us see why clients make the decisions they do. For example, a house your clients called home for twenty years will have value to that couple that has nothing to do with its worth. The marks on the doorframes and dings in the floor have stories attached to them, each happy memory increases value. So, during the financial crisis of 2008, homes that dropped in worth from $500,000 to $300,000 maintained their value.

Balancing the concept of value versus worth with clients can be tricky for Total Relationship Advisors. Clients inevitably assign value to their assets regardless of their worth—even investments. A client's most prized stock may be worth the least. Advisors need to remember the only way that the worth of an investment goes down is by selling shares when the price drops.

This circles back to the half-truths in the old adage of buy low and sell high. Advisors often assume we sell high because the value of the stock will max out and drop, and we buy only when the price is low because it can only increase in worth. However, in that scenario, we turn our attention to not selling too early or buying too soon because the stock could continue to rise or fall. We forget that the intrinsic value of the future of that company determines the investment's ultimate value. A stock of low worth or one that drops after a spike in price could produce a nice steady income over decades making it quite valuable. Looking at an overview of the last fifty years, I would argue that most things have lost half their worth but increased in value.

Panic can set in when clients start to focus on what they should be holding or buying. But the Total Relationship Advisor who fully understands the difference between current worth and long-term value helps clients avoid those mistakes. Advisors become teachers as we educate clients, and as they begin to understand the difference between worth and value, they learn to trust us even more. I saw this with a client named Lucas.

Lucas worked hard in his roofing business based in Chicago. He had lost the first million he made when he was swindled by someone he trusted. The bad deal forced him to start from scratch in a different area because his partner turned on him.

Despite this, Lucas always had a smile on his face. He was a great saver and loved cheap, quick, little cars. Before the financial crisis of 2008, Lucas had built a two-million-dollar nest egg. We had just come out of the prosperous tech bubble, and that year the market cut nearly every portfolio in half. We spent the next two to three years building them back. My firm lost three clients during that challenging time, and Lucas was one of them.

Lucas and the others couldn't handle the portfolio downturn and believed changing advisors would make a difference. Other downturns had taught me that when the market goes through a crisis like that, investors shouldn't rush to sell. Thus, I always try to talk a client out of liquidating their portfolio when things look bleakest.

If after three meetings, I can't help them understand the benefits of sticking with our plan through the tough years, I allow them to make the decision to change their portfolio. However, during each meeting, I explain my Three-Strike system which says after the third attempt of trying to save the clients from themselves, I will do what they want. This often means liquidating the portfolio. It also means I will resign as their advisor. Three meetings allows time for emotions to calm and facts to bring clarity on the differences between wealth and value. I do not want to be responsible for taking a client out of a portfolio that I have confidence will eventually flourish. So, I encourage them to find an advisor that works with their investing philosophy.

Behavioral Finance teaches us that clients who leave their investments out of panic feel good about their decision as the markets decline. However, their decision causes them to miss the buy lower opportunities. It is not until the market recovers and moves higher than the client's panic point that the client's FoMO takes charge. Then they want to buy back in. Often the result of preventing a temporary decline in value creates a permanent loss of opportunity. Additionally, the advisor who allows this to happen is responsible for getting them out and getting them back in when doing nothing would have often been the better option.

Total Relationship Advisors counsel and try to protect clients from themselves. We work hard to prevent clients from making choices based on feelings. Emotions run high and fast and will often shift with the market, but emotion-based investing will nearly always cause loss and hardship in the end.

Before Lucas and I had our third meeting, he called and said, "Tyson, sometimes they gotta fire the head coach when they don't win the Superbowl." He went on to explain that he was going to find a new advisor he thought could manage his portfolio better. I replied, "Okay, Lucas. The door is always open. You know where I stand on this, but I wish you well." Everyone on the team signed a handwritten note thanking him for being our client, and that was, for the time being, the end of our relationship with Lucas.

A true Total Relationship Advisor keeps the door open. He or she makes a client's departure as pleasant as their onboarding to make sure the client knows they will always be welcome back should that occasion ever present itself.

Over a decade later, Lucas called again to ask me to look over his portfolio. I told him I would be happy to help. When he came to the office, he handed me a portfolio worth almost exactly the same as when he left our firm. He wanted to know why his portfolio hadn't grown. As I looked through his statements, I noticed that half of his investments had a fixed rate, giving him about 2% growth over the decade. During that same period diversified portfolios had achieved almost a double-digit rate of return.

Lucas knew others who had enjoyed that diversified growth, so he was confused. "How did this happen, Tyson?"

The answer was simple. The advisor he had chosen to replace me ten years ago did exactly what he asked. "Lucas, when you told the new advisor you didn't like the market and didn't want to lose anymore, they appeased you. He gave you what you asked for, not necessarily what was best over the long haul."

Unfortunately, when the market shifted and started doing well again, this new advisor didn't ask Lucas if he wanted to move back to a growth-minded portfolio, so his investments remained nearly stagnant for a decade. And some of the strategies they used essentially trapped him in low earning investments because they sold with no commission upfront but had declining penalties if they were liquidated over the next fifteen years.

Lucas and his daughter finally began to see the difference between value and worth. While his portfolio dropped in worth momentarily when the market declined, the overall value would have continued to increase had he weathered the market as we suggested. Additionally, Lucas felt firsthand the repercussions of what happens when financial advisors appease their clients. I believe appeasement is a different form of neglect; clients need investors that can grow their income over multiple decades, and liquidating portfolios as a knee jerk reaction to a declining market is a disservice. Like Lucas, learning the difference between value and worth the hard way is something many clients have to do, but being the guiding voice of reason is a key responsibility of the Total Relationship Advisor.

ACCUMULATING RICHES VERSUS THE STEWARDSHIP OF WEALTH

As we transform our mindset from simply grappling for more into the Total Relationship, we need to contrast two words. Riches and wealth are often used interchangeably and have similar definitions. Used in the context of financial advising, however, we need to emphasize the difference.

When we hear the word rich, we usually think more. But Total Relationship Advisors look for meaning, not more. We want to shift the focus of our clients from riches to the stewardship of wealth. Being good stewards of our wealth lets us experience life to its fullest in the happiest way possible.

The word stewardship has its roots in the person who took care of his master's belongings. A good steward was the most valuable servant on the estate and in very ancient times might have inherited part of the estate if the master lacked heirs.

Clients come to us looking for someone to help them achieve their unique goals. Forward-thinking in nature, goals encourage us to look ahead. Our job is to suggest a plan that will take care of the wealth so that those goals can come to fruition.

As necessary as they are, goals can also become a stumbling block. Performance driven individuals learn to move quickly from achievement to achievement. They tend to keep moving the goalpost forward. The mentality of always seeking more, pushing ahead without purpose or meaning, leads to the get-rich mindset. These individuals lose the ability to be content in their current space. They only see what they can get and miss the beauty of the moment as well as the lessons of the past.

Conversely, those who have learned to be good stewards of their wealth are aware of where they have come from, what they have now, and where they would like their wealth to take them. Appreciating the journey is essential to living a full life. Wealth stewardship embraces the idea that to move ahead you have to know where you came from. This mentality keeps us from getting caught up in the more rather than searching for true meaning.

A riches-seeking client tends to have feelings tied to unpredictable trends, allowing out of control situations to control them entirely. Some try to show off their riches which often leads to unnecessary debt. In their quest for accumulation, these individuals often spend money they don't have, buying boats, cars, and more in an attempt, as the old adage goes, to keep up with the Joneses. Unfortunately, there will always be a new, better, more expensive Jones family living on the block. In constantly seeking more, clients attempting to get rich are seldom looking for contentment. They don't even understand the concept. They care more about possessions than they do about themselves.

Clients who have learned wealth stewardship exhibit the opposite behavior. They typically manage their money well and buy things that bring joy for themselves and those they deeply care about. Regardless of their cash flow, they never use their money for show. Clients who understand wealth stewardship intentionally search for meaning. They are anxious to share their formation story and know where they want to go. Plus, their planning prepares them for comfort and contentment in their retirement years.

Back in 2004, I met a widow who became a prospective client shortly after the 2008 recession. The woman had a net worth of $40 million and came to me in extreme panic as the stock market plummeted. I explained we could help her regain much of her portfolio, or at the very least we could review it and reinvest, but her alarm made her want to pull the account immediately. At the time, I didn't yet understand the difference between riches and wealth stewardship, so I missed the fact that this woman was chasing finances and fighting to protect the riches she had accumulated. Though her net worth remained in the millions even in the midst of great loss, she couldn't be content.

Our conversation began with her telling me about the incredibly heavy sadness and suffering she carried. I straightened, prepared to comfort her on the loss of her husband or some other incredibly difficult trial. I was taken aback when instead she began to list everything she owned and the money she had that fueled her seemingly unending misery. She spoke about the way her possessions controlled her life. They consumed her thinking; and working on how to keep them or how to get more drove her.

This woman is just one example of hundreds who have so much that it takes over their lives and replaces everything they care about. Those seeking riches become so fixated on possessing more that they don't own anything; the material things own them. They don't even realize their possessions have stolen their peace and left them with loneliness and anxiety.

As advisors, we should seek to fund our clients' contentment. This means helping them find their satisfaction threshold. Every person has a point where continuing to add assets no longer increases contentment.

Though different for each client, all will eventually reach it. This marks the point in the discussion when we introduce options that will not only keep their money safe, but also add joy and meaning to their lives.

Great advisors aspire to prevent the riches mentality or the mindset of accumulation. Advisors who choose to help their clients discover the joy of wealth stewardship reap rewards when they see tangible changes in the lives of people they care about. Shifting our focus from riches to people allows for deeper contentment, not only in the lives of our clients but in our lives as well. We become more satisfied with our roles when we see them living joy-filled lives.

I feel fulfilled when our practice helps a client create a beautiful legacy. The stewardship of wealth philosophy gets passed on when children watch their parents work their dream job–a career chosen out of passion not paycheck. I want to be the kind of advisor who counts the memories made on family vacations, the children added to the family, and the laughter and joyful moments healthy investments bring rather than the commas in the ledger.

Breaking these molds means a change in mindsets for advisors as well as clients. Providing clients with a wealth stewardship mentality rather than a riches mindset allows them to make a continual impact for years to come. Meaning, rather than more, defines the value of the legacies we leave behind.

SECTION TWO:

PARTNERSHIP FORMATION

CHAPTER THREE:

FORMING TRUST

Planning for your financial future means focusing on long-term investing, and those that take the time to map out the direction of their life can be tremendously successful. Unfortunately, the constant bombardment of day-to-day, minute-by-minute information proves distracting. The world prefers to focus on the now and disregards future plans in exchange for current fun. However, the world has no destination in mind, and without a target, they wander lost without even realizing.

DESTINATION OR DISTRACTION

Let's consider what the rest of life looks like if we compare it to a long road trip that includes all four corners of the continental United States. If we start on Highway One and make our way from Maine to Florida, Highway

One represents the first two decades of our lives—our education and growth years. When we arrive in Florida, we stop for a moment to relax and enjoy spring break.

After a short breather, we travel Interstate 10 from Florida to California. This is one of the two longest parts of our journey. We leave the youthful experiences of Florida and move through the heat and mountains. This leg of the trip represents our career, and like those years in life, sometimes the beauty of the trip will outweigh the troubles, and other times we'll feel like we've hit a desert. We may have as many jobs as states, or one career may span the entire length.

The journey from Southern California to Washington begins when we start thinking about retirement. If we took our trip seriously, we stopped for an oil change and prepared for this leg of the journey while we were on Interstate 10. Some of our traversing will be enjoyable, but we'll hit storms along the way. Hopefully, we prepared before we hit Arizona so we're ready for setbacks.

The final leg of our trip takes us from Washington to Maine and represents the future we started planning for before we began the journey. These miles will be at least as long as our career jaunt, but we'll be able to enjoy the scenery a bit more if we've planned well.

Like our long-trip metaphor, a map makes it easier to plan. We can look down the road and ask questions as we go. We get to make the decision about where we want to be and how many years we want to travel. We account for detours and scenic routes that might cause us to diverge from our original plan. Just like road construction, car troubles, and temporary distractions can change our route, job changes, illness, and children's adventures may get us off course a bit.

We have to be careful when we take the momentary exit ramp. What we had determined to be a tiny break reveals billboards tempting us to take a direction that has nothing to do with our planned journey through life.

Every decision we make offers the same distractions—so many sites to see and things to do. Each obstacle, mountain, and unexpected detour tempts us to stray from our plan. But if we don't stick to it, our drive from Washington to Maine will be rough, if not impossible.

Just like a long road trip, you can't feed short-term information into your long-term decisions. Short-term information leads to *distraction* not *direction.* Long-term investing means creating a plan for the rest of your life. However, life happens, and adjustments become necessary. Without a professional to guide us through these times, the change can breed fear and become signs along the road tempting us to move away from our plan. These signs can seem overwhelming, but when you're in a multi-decade financial plan, you have to ignore them. We can't allow ourselves to be distracted.

When we hear about returns and the day-to-day movements of the market, it's important to remember these are merely placards that long-term investors should ignore. The only thing that matters on long-distance road trips is where you are relative to your destination. Are you heading in the right direction? Everything else is irrelevant. In investing, this constant barrage of information begs long-term investors to change their strategy and to change it now. But long-term investors are not trying to make decisions for their investments today. That's what we use cash for.

So, what options do amateur investors have? They could do it themselves, and many try. They find their own maps and plan their rest stops, but until they take that final off-ramp, the wisdom of their choices won't be clear. Alternately, amateurs could choose to hire a professional to guide and assist them in understanding which signs are critical to arriving at the destination, and which are merely distractions.

Rather than allowing clients to drive alone or assigning them a chauffeur, trustworthy financial advisors stay as close as the backseat. We help the investor navigate the course, keep them on the correct highway, and let them know when getting off to see the sites is the best choice.

Having an understanding of short-term versus long-term investing on both sides is the first building block to a Total Relationship with clients. When advisors don't allow short-term distractions to alter the long-term destination, it builds an element of trust with clients and will pay off when their drive from Washington to Maine is peaceful and scenic. It is crucial that clients know we are with them for the long-haul if we expect them to put their full trust in us.

INSTANT VERSUS INTENTIONAL

With each new client, advisors need to keep in mind we are forming trusting relationships that will evolve over time. As the relationship grows, so will the communication about the client's life, well-being, and goals. Phone calls will go back and forth, and advisors have to choose the kind of phone call we want each one to be—instant or intentional.

The instant call is also what we call the feel-good phone call. It gives the allusion of establishing trust and building a solid foundation for a future relationship because it starts on a positive note. Instantly, we set up an affirmative connection between advisor and client that makes both sides feel good. However, despite its tremendous beginning, this is merely surface-level trust, and it would be tragic if we mistake this instant connection for a deeper relationship.

The intentional call creates a substantially deeper relationship but takes more effort and has potential risks. The Total Relationship emerges when we demonstrate integrity and show interest in a relationship that's intentional, not instant. It involves difficult conversations and painful truths. Some clients will reject our advice. Not everyone likes brutal honesty, regardless of how professionally you frame it. Consistency and care will foster Total Relationships, so when a client comes looking for an instant connection and quick solutions rather than intentional relationships and plans, we must exercise patience.

In my first years of financial advising, I took on a client named Mr. Martin. He had a substantial portfolio and felt frustrated at its slow growth. Looking at his statements, I saw that he had essentially doubled his portfolio in a small amount of time, but the growth had become stagnant. After reviewing his investments, I suggested we take some of his profit and use it to deleverage a percentage of his debt.

Initially, Mr. Martin hated the idea. He raised three essential concerns: his position in the market, my commission, and the taxes on his withdrawals. Instead of using appeasement to create an instant relationship with Mr. Martin, I vocalized my rationale and pushed back against his opposition. To build an intentional relationship, I had to tell my client that his decision to continue on the path he was on was incredibly risky.

Despite my relationship building efforts, Mr. Martin opted to continue with his portfolio in its current position. We had that difficult conversation a few times, and I resolved to stick to my stance with integrity while still doing my best to support him.

Time passed and Mr. Martin's account dipped to nearly thirty percent of its original equity. He had either to bring in more money or sell his positions to cover the loss. I tracked his bank balances watching him put thousands into his portfolio in an attempt to make up the losses while it continued to decline rapidly.

During this time, I continued to have those honest, intentional conversations with him. One of the hardest calls came when his wife informed me that he mortgaged his house in order to keep his portfolio. The very next week the market dropped another ten percent, and his entire portfolio was nearly gone. Mr. Martin would be paying off his house for the next thirty years if something didn't change. Another ten percent drop the next week, and his mortgage deposit was lost. He had effectively gone from a two-million-dollar portfolio to a twenty-thousand-dollar portfolio in a matter of months.

Despite how sickening it was to watch an entire portfolio be destroyed, sticking with my decision to build an intentional relationship was reinforced by a different call I received from Mr. Martin's wife. She explained how thankful she was that the portfolio had hit rock bottom. Not only did she finally have her husband back, but she also knew she could fully trust me with their money. I could have supported Mr. Martin in his risky decision-making and built an instant relationship. Instead, I chose to push back to develop an intentional, long-term relationship. When things turned south, I was still there to support him with the difficult things he didn't want to hear.

Every new client offers these options, and we continually get to decide which kind of relationship to build. We can make them feel good, or we can tell them the truth which may or may not be pleasant. It's a matter of instant connection or intentional connection.

Mr. Martin saw my intentionality was genuine from the beginning. His trust in me didn't come because of a great profit. He put his trust in me because I earned it. The Total Relationship is based on this foundation of trust, and in order to keep fostering it, we must pick the more difficult of the two connections.

CHAPTER FOUR:

THE PARTNERSHIP EVERY CLIENT NEEDS

As you've already seen, a Total Relationship Advisor becomes so much more than just a money manager. The trust that develops in this relationship allows you to move into even more roles in your clients' lives. Three of the most important roles in this relationship are those of teacher, coach, and advocate.

BECOMING THE TEACHER

When a client comes to us, they need help, and we can begin with giving them a bit of education on financial security. They don't necessarily need to know the ins and outs of how we plan to invest their money. Nor do they need a crash course on the inner workings of the stock market. Rather, many clients need a lesson in the role money plays in their lives and how that information has the potential to shape their lives.

We begin by educating them regarding the limited resources at their disposal–especially time, energy, and money. Consider our scenic drive analogy—when traveling from one point to another, we have a limited amount of time. We want to get through the mountains before the February snows. Likewise, clients need to develop an awareness of that limited time. Twenty-year-olds tend to think they'll live forever, and as we help people see that retirement or health issues will be there before they know it, they begin to approach money management with a deliberate reality. Helping our clients learn how time impacts their choices teaches them a lifelong skill that will enable them to become experts at prioritizing their life goals.

Similarly, energy conservation is incredibly important. Our clients often don't realize how much energy we devote to the things and people around us. They don't think of energy as a limited resource like time or money. But the truth is we only have so much mental space and physical energy to devote to projects, people, and goals. Even those who recognize the need to go green and conserve energy often don't understand the importance of protecting their mental or physical energy. By teaching our clients that principle, we help them prioritize. Understanding the concept of limited time and energy will help our clients fully grasp why we invest as we do and why they should trust us.

Most obviously, our job as advisors is to teach our clients about the limited resource of money without putting them into a scarcity mindset. Stories can be a powerful tool to explain ideas to clients. When we share our personal experience, we can also develop a deeper connection. Telling stories is one of my favorite ways to help clients understand what is happening with their money.

Unlike energy and time, most people already view money as a limited resource. Therefore, our emphasis will be how we can increase the resources they currently have to create a scarcity-free future.

Understanding limits helps the average person prioritize the way they spend these valuable resources. In fact, treating these commodities as limited can actually multiply them. As clients begin to understand their finiteness, they make decisions that conserve energy, multiply finances, and make every moment count.

Taking on the role of the teacher as we begin to build relationships is essential to creating the trust that forms the ultimate Total Relationship. Clients gain confidence when advisors showcase their knowledge in a way that proves helpful and educational. We customize the education based on what matters to the client. Too many advisors try to teach clients everything they know about investments and the markets when many clients don't want or need that kind of knowledge. Instead, we help them understand how investing can give them a better life as well as the importance of keeping their focus on what matters to them now and for their future.

We also try to bring clients to the realization they do not need to know or focus on every bit of information out there. Clients don't need to waste time or energy trying to learn something that adds no benefit to their lives. When clients see that we understand their situation, they are much more inclined to have faith in our abilities.

BECOME THE COACH

Understanding the difference between coach and teacher can be difficult at times, but it boils down to the way we use our knowledge. Teachers primarily share new information and help students begin to implement the lessons. Coaches, on the other hand, focus on developing and refining information or skills. Once they've learned the lessons, we can move from teacher to coach.

Financial coaching begins much like life coaching. Both kinds of advisors use their first meetings to ask questions that help us understand our clients' specific needs and positions. I like to start with these three broad questions that can become highly specific to each individual client.

1. Where do you want to go?
2. What do you want to do?
3. Who do you want to be?

After our clients understand what it means to have limited resources, they will be able to answer these questions well and with purpose. A financial coach directs clients to take time and think extensively about these questions. He also lets them know the answers to these questions may need to be revised as they grow and change. The answers allow advisors to analyze and respond accordingly.

Once we understand what the client wants from the relationship, coaching can transform the connection into the Total Relationship. Coaches know their players; they recognize strengths and weaknesses and can identify their players' skills. Knowing our client's strengths, weaknesses, and skills allows us to create strategic plans that help clients take what they already know and craft it into what they want their money to become.

How does coaching play into our aim of developing intentional trust with our clients? Players trust their coaches. They trust them to make play calls and to set up the team for success as much as possible. In the Total Relationship, the advisor and the client are exactly that:

a team. We've seen how the relationship functions in a teacher/student fashion, and now we can see how it will work in a coach/player fashion. When clients see that we make their goals our focus, they trust our ideas and plans as we coach them through the game of life.

Coaching is a fantastic way to build an intentional relationship instead of an instant one. As we walk through life with our clients, they will see that over time their goals begin to play out when they listen to our coaching. It is the job of the coach to take what the clients already know about themselves and create a life plan that keeps them focused on that goal.

BECOMING THE ADVOCATE

The final role of a Total Relationship Advisor is that of advocate. Unlike teaching and coaching, advocating for clients calls for a deeper care and understanding of our clients as people. The primary responsibility of an advocate is support. On the surface or in an instant relationship that may look like simply keeping track of positions and assets, as all advisors do.

Supporting clients in the Total Relationship means that advisors seek to bring meaning, motivation, and empowerment to the wealth they are building and preserving. This means that when we ask about the client's goals, we dig until we understand the why of those goals. Knowing the why behind the goal enables us to move from teacher and coach to advocate.

Advocating for our clients includes asking about their past and how they've come to be who they are. Advising looks different for each client depending on their answers to those questions. Regardless of these answers, in order to properly advocate, the financial advisor and client must truly connect. Once we understand who they are, where they've come from and where they want to go, we can advocate for their happiness by working with them on continuing, and in some cases reinventing, their life plans.

For clients to develop a deeper level of trust with advisors, it's necessary for them to think of advisors as advocates. Total Relationship Advisors understand the line between advocate and friend. He or she has one goal in mind: supporting their clients to help them achieve their goals and happiness as much as possible. Advocates don't worry about hurt feelings or tense moments because bringing clients back from detours is an absolute necessity if we want to move our clients from where they are to where they want to be.

Clients see an advisor's commitment to them when the advisor advocates vocally and consistently. Trust is built over time—not instantly, but intentionally. A Total Relationship Advisor will remain his or her clients' biggest advocates through demanding times or unexpected circumstances. They develop confidence in the Total Relationship, rather than market patterns or financial victories. Advocating for our clients becomes the most essential aspect and the foundational role in the Total Relationship Approach. Most essential because when the advisor understands the why behind what the client wants, the recommendation can and may require going against everything we've been taught or coached. Sometimes decisions for the best life won't follow the guidelines for the best financial decision. In fact, they may need to go against the plan. The advocate-advisor has the wisdom to know the difference and recommend accordingly.

This triad of roles produces an advisor committed to creating an intentional relationship with clients. It takes dedication and a vested interest in more than just the well-being of their money. The advocate advisor also looks after the well-being of the person.

Total Relationship Advisors will teach an understanding of limited resources, coach clients through the ups and downs of investing, and advocate for their happiness and their goals through persistent commitment and communication.

CHAPTER FIVE:

PARTNERSHIP BENEFITS

I truly enjoy partnering with clients to help them live their best life. Though my primary objective is to educate, coach, and advocate while we build our relationship, my job has become a joy because, through the Total Relationship Approach, I get to see the beauty this partnership can bring.

PARTNERSHIP BEGINS BY ASKING THE RIGHT QUESTIONS

Having a solid understanding of who our clients are is the most pivotal part of the Total Relationship. Most advisors enter the juncture by asking clients to fill out a questionnaire. While this sounds like a solid beginning and a way to gather pertinent information quickly, the practice can lead to instant connection rather than intentional relationship. Typical, government-esque questionnaires are a deceptively easy answer to a much deeper need.

Most questionnaires contain seemingly helpful, risk-analyzing questions; however, they omit an important element. They include tick boxes rather than space for clients to tell their stories. Checkboxes and a sliding scale use a formula to spit out the best course of action. It doesn't take the unique problems and dreams of each client into consideration. Long term interests, needs, and desires can be easily overlooked.

These questionnaires are designed to gauge an understanding of a client's risk tolerance. Yet when we ask the question, "What is your willingness to lose money?" isn't everyone's honest answer, "None"?

These questionnaires forget that clients don't fit into a neat box. They ignore the fact we deal with real people trying to live their lives and enjoy their freedoms while still making wise choices for the future. In order to find out what that looks like for each client, the answers need to be more than simply A, B, C, or all of the above. Open-ended questions offer a better way to let advisors see the full picture of who the client is and how to move forward.

When we balance these open-ended questions with the fundamentals, we can create a portfolio that matches our client. Markets will fluctuate, and the advisor will need to remind the client how they felt about their portfolios when a decline wasn't driving their emotions. We can use their stories to help them remember that day when they answered important questions that helped them make logical and fundamental decisions for their future.

The weight of stories over checkmarks became most evident to me in a most unusual place.

Mr. Decani took me under his wing as an apprentice when I started in the business. He taught me everything I needed to know about getting to know clients and what success looked like in the finance industry.

During my second year as a junior advisor, I learned how little I actually knew about a client. I believed I had gotten to know him well, but at Floyd's funeral, I learned differently.

My office in William's firm was tiny, what you might expect for an apprentice. With no windows, no door, and essentially no privacy, I looked forward to the day when I would have more than a cubicle.

One day, Mr. Decani interrupted my work, knocking assertively on the wall. He told me to grab my jacket, and we headed out into the brisk spring morning.

The snow had melted and the leaves from fall still littered the ground. The air felt warm after the harsh winter. As we walked out of the office, I turned toward

Mr. Decani's car, but he kept walking. We continued for about two blocks, took a left, and found ourselves on the sidewalk outside of the Dutch Reformed Church. I was confused about why we were there until I saw the placard "Funeral Service Today for Floyd Smith. . ."

I sat down in the back pew and took in the crowd. I didn't know a single soul in the building. Mr. Decani, on the other hand, flitted from person to person; he seemed to know everyone. He spoke to them naturally and with such familiarity that I was sure Floyd must have been a family friend or close acquaintance.

The service began, and Mr. Decani found me. I listened to the hymns and the message, and then Floyd's friends and family began speaking. For twenty or thirty minutes people shared cherished memories. One after another they stood and told of wonderful times spent together. Despite not knowing Floyd, I felt moved by the passion of his admirers and wished I had known him better myself, so I could fully understand the pain they felt.

After the service, I grabbed my jacket, and we began walking back to the office. Mr. Decani looked at me and said, "So, what did you learn?"

I replied with a question of my own, "About the business or about Floyd?"

"They are one and the same," he replied, continuing to walk at a comfortable pace. "Tell me what you learned."

I told him that I learned how much Floyd's family and friends loved him, that he had three children, all girls, and was active in his career and in the church. I was impressed by the number of the people who spoke about him who were coworkers and members of his congregation. I learned Floyd loved bowling and bowled a perfect game three times in his lifetime. I learned that he enjoyed spending time up north on the lake, fishing for bass and muskies. Plus, I learned that he was crazy in college and even crazier in his age of retirement. It seemed like Floyd was great at making people laugh.

When I finished, Mr. Decani smiled and said, "That's the success of our business. You didn't hear those people talk about how we helped Floyd save for retirement or how we helped him buy the lake house and the fishing boat in Sugar Camp he always wanted. No one said a word about cash flows, whether or not he paid for his kids' college education or how we made sure he never ran out of money. No, they share their memories and joyful moments, all the things that happened because we worked behind the scenes to help Floyd live the best life possible. We allowed Floyd to be in the moment 100% of the time because he trusted us with his finances. That is what it means to be successful in this industry, Tyson."

Until that day, I had no idea that Floyd loved being up north or that his favorite beer was Spotted Cow. Mr.

Decani taught me what might be the most important and counter-intuitive lesson in the finance world. Success is not about money; it's about knowing the people we work with well enough to help them achieve more than they even realized they wanted. It took attending a funeral to see that Floyd and every client we served were more than checked boxes and the numbers and percentages in their portfolios.

As I reflected on all the time I had spent cultivating clients and convincing myself that I knew them based on yes or no boxes, I began to recognize my naivety in believing that I could learn enough from a questionnaire, a quick conversation, and the small talk in the annual meetings to truly understand the best way to serve them.

After my experience with Floyd, I gradually changed my approach to client onboarding. I realized I was not asking the right questions. In fact, I barely asked any questions at all. I had been operating under the assumption that clients wanted me to handle their money, not tell me their stories. That funeral helped me see that a financial advisor cannot truly handle a client's money with purpose and intentionality if he or she does not know that client's story.

Asking the right kinds of questions will ultimately lead to the most successful client/advisor relationships in the industry. I've grown genuinely to love asking open-ended questions that give clients the opportunity to share the high and low moments of their lives as well as where they are now and where they want to end up. It is not about more money. It is about a better life—a life lived fully right to the end. Listening to what our clients have done, are doing, and want to do helps us open doors for them. Often, with the right questions, a listening ear, and proper investing, we can take the dream of a fishing cabin on Lake Superior and turn it into that plus a fishing adventure across multiple countries. Listening and learning creates a Total Relationship that fully understands how to help make our clients' lives bountiful and successful so they can live out their wildest dreams.

PEOPLE, NOT PRODUCTS - MORE VERSUS MEANING

On a bitterly cold evening during the first week of December of 2001, we held an open house to celebrate the new office. As the junior advisor, they put me in charge of invitations. I sent one to every address in our database which unexpectedly included clients with closed and low asset accounts.

Celebratory balloons and tables of food lined the freshly painted, soft gray walls. Nearly everyone invited came. Champagne, smiles, and chats about business ventures and the weather highlighted the lively evening.

As I mingled, I noticed one guest looked out of place. The woman piled her plate high with hors d'oeuvres and fresh veggies. Curious, I asked the senior partner and several of our assistants if they happened to know the mysterious woman, but no one seemed to recognize her.

I approached her confidently and introduced myself as the new branch manager. She balanced her plate and politely shook my hand.,

"Hello, I'm Virginia."

"So nice to meet you, Virginia. What do you think of the new office?"

She nodded, looking around the room thoughtfully. "I like it. It looks nice," she finally replied.

"Thank you for coming, if there is anything we can help you with, please let me know."

"Actually, yes. I have a few questions about investments and probate. Could we set up a time to talk about it?"

A week later, Virginia sat opposite me and pulled a piece of paper from her purse. Sliding it across my desk, she asked flippantly, "Is this worth anything?"

A stock certificate for 5000 shares of Enron stared back at me. Just a few weeks prior, that piece of paper would have been worth over half a million dollars, but Enron's bankruptcy announcement had rendered it essentially worthless. I softly shared the unwelcome news, as she nodded in understanding, "Yes, that's what I thought."

Her unphased demeanor seemed strange and almost awkward.

"Do you have more of these?" I asked as I handed back her Enron Stock certificate.

She leaned in, almost with a twinkle in her eye, and replied "Yeah, I have a lot of them." She explained that she had bought shares in a variety of companies over the years, I told her we needed to check them all before another company she had invested in went bankrupt. At our next meeting, Virginia brought in a laundry basket of old stock certificates and dividend reinvestment reports. As we investigated Virginia's stocks, we counted fifty she had accumulated over fifty years of investing.

Virginia's collection, which some mistakenly confuse with a portfolio, included many investments that, like Enron, were essentially worthless. As we talked through each one, I asked how she selected these companies to put her trust in.

Virginia worked in a library in a nearby town. She related that her late husband had owned a utility company until it had been bought out by another company. After countless other buyouts, Enron eventually owned the company that had at one time belonged to Virginia's husband. That inspired Virginia to purchase her first stocks. After that, she did research on the library computers and bought shares whenever she was able.

As we worked to salvage Virginia's account, we also discovered that despite the number of worthless assets, she had just a few profitable holdings. While this story shows the power of long-term investments, it also demonstrates something not as pleasant.

Though I had the privilege of telling her she was a multi-millionaire, I quickly realized the eighty-year-old librarian didn't understand the implications.

"I know; I have been told that before." Virginia explained that other advisors had reviewed her holdings, but she never trusted anyone to help her. They had been a lot more excited about the value of the stocks than I was.

"Okay, can I ask a question?"

She nodded

"How much do you make a month as a librarian?"

She looked surprised. And as she paused, I thought, *She just showed her multi-million dollar account, but she doesn't want to tell me how much she makes a month as a librarian.*

Embarrassed, she said, "About $5,000 a month." Then she quickly followed that up with, "I know it is a lot of money, but I have been there for 50 years."

Smiling inside, I glossed over that and asked the next question, "If I could show you that you have enough to replace the $5,000 a month, would you retire from being a librarian?"

I spent the next thirty minutes showing her how we could turn off the dividend reinvestment option and create enough cash flow for her to retire. In the next few weeks, we consolidated, diversified, and built her a portfolio allowing her to retire. She trusted me because I helped her see I wasn't focused on how much but rather what for.

The financial advising industry tends to focus on numbers. How many dollars have been invested, gained, or lost? How many clients do we have? But advisors have a more essential role. Despite the pressure to keep adding tick marks to the counter, we need to keep in mind we are not after more. Mindsets based on acquiring the largest numbers need to be abandoned because the numbers game inevitably results in treating clients as products.

'Clients are people, not products' needs to become the advisor's mantra. These valuable people have stories, desires, hopes, and dreams. When we shift our mindset to remember this, we develop a full understanding of what motivates them. Without hearing the stories and understanding the motivation behind their investments, we won't fully understand how best to work for them. Virginia's story helped me see her greatest priorities—hard work, dedication, and perseverance—which enabled me to establish estate and investment strategies in a fashion that made her life better, giving her a retirement she could have had twenty years earlier.

People search for meaning not more. When our advisor-client relationships enhance life's meaning rather than build more with products, we move from an old model relationship to the Total Relationship.

GIVE YOUR CLIENTS PERMISSION TO LIVE

Unfortunately, many people believe advisors should be focused on saving or making more money for clients. And while saving money as we prepare for the future must be one of our goals, if that money never gets spent, what good is it?

Because money is so closely tied to the quality of life and a feeling of security, it's difficult to move past a riches mentality. Advisors have a responsibility to take into consideration the physical limitations their clients may face if they make saving for retirement their only goal. That meaningful-life mindset only happens when advisors excel in something we touched on in previous chapters—the permission business.

Clients have a naturally embedded fear of spending. Fear of future scarcity causes them to live in present scarcity. They've worked hard to save to make a comfortable future, so they hesitate to use that money for today. We will meet people who need reined-in, but more often we'll find clients who need someone willing to step in and give them permission to spend their hard-earned money on living life now. Allowing them to continue in this scarcity mindset incurs the greatest risk—a life not lived.

I learned this lesson from a woman named Joyce in my first year as an advisor. In her late eighties, Joyce was physically impaired and unable to drive. One sunny day, I drove to Joyce's house with the intention of finding out what direction she wanted to take her portfolio. The twenty-four-year-old me plopped down at her kitchen table and began making small talk. I quickly learned she had no kids, but many close nieces and nephews. Her late husband, Roger, an incredibly frugal man, had died nearly twenty years before. Her husband's example resulted in Joyce never spending their investments for fear of losing it, or worse, wasting it.

Looking at her multi-million-dollar portfolio, I asked her "What do you want to do with your investments?"

She shrugged and said, "However Roger left it, that's the way it should stay. I don't want to mess anything up."

"What's this money for then?"

She paused for a moment, "At this point in my life, I don't really know. I can't drive or get around without my walker. That money is only black ink on white paper to me. The numbers change every quarter, but nothing changes for me."

"Has anyone ever asked you about this before?"

"No, not really," she replied.

Social security and her husband's pension gave Joyce a comfortable life, but she had millions of dollars tucked away that could have given her and Roger some wonderful memories from the last several decades. No one had ever given her permission to live the life she wanted.

Over the next few years, I visited Joyce several times. Our small talk always led to reminiscing. She shared stories of the trips she and Roger had taken and the gifts she had given her nieces and nephews. But she also told me about all the things she wished she had done. Her list included a trip to Paris to see the Eiffel Tower, a visit to the World War Two memorials, and owning a beach condo. She could have easily done all those things had someone only given her permission.

When we think about giving our clients permission, it's good to ask about their bucket list. If money was no object, what would you do? What trips would you take? What would you buy? Encouraging clients to dream and create a list of at least ten things they know they want to accomplish helps us do our jobs. It empowers advisors to create a plan that will give clients permission to live life now and still achieve their retirement goals.

Helping clients to see they can afford to live their best lives can be as simple as showing them they have everything they need to be satisfied; they don't need to continue striving for more and more. We can ponder, dream, and hope for a better future. And while we should never give up on our dreams, sometimes we have to adjust to the next turn in the road. Change is part of life, and it is important to be able to adapt and appreciate what you already have. In fact, it can be difficult to truly achieve the future of our dreams until we learn to appreciate what we have in the present.

As Total Relationship Advisors, it's our job to ask clients if they enjoy their current opportunities and lifestyle. Many have saved and invested for years waiting for "someday" to give them a bigger and brighter tomorrow. Yet, all the time, everything they always wanted is right in front of them. All they have to do is slow down and take hold. Retirement is often the opportunity to enjoy what is already in front of them, but some don't even realize it. Too often our clients will feel they need to work more, do more, and never spend. My job, and the responsibility of all Total Relationship Advisors, is to help people see and enjoy every opportunity. After they've run the race and made all the correct adjustments to changes in family, careers, and the markets, we simply need to give them permission to enjoy all they've worked for.

Removing clients from the constant-hustle mentality that is so embedded in the American work culture can be difficult. We can count it a success when we help clients understand that they worked hard, so they can enjoy the luxuries of life. Offering permission to enjoy the rewards of their labor brings an abundance to their lives that otherwise may have never surfaced.

PROTECTING CLIENTS FROM THEMSELVES

Giving clients permission to live and helping them enjoy a life of true wealth also means, to a certain extent, we are protecting them from themselves. Finances tend to cause knee-jerk reactions. Fear drives people to save and never spend and causes them to trade pursuit of their passion for future security or safety.

I worked as an advisor for an anesthesiologist named Matt. Matt's parents grew up during the great depression. They impressed upon him the need to save more than any client I've ever had. Though he had saved enough to retire at sixty-five, he continued to work until sixty-six, then sixty-seven. As Matt neared seventy, I spent most of our meetings attempting to point out tactfully that money is no longer his most precious resource, time is.

Matt finally retired at seventy-two. He and his wife decided to take an international vacation to celebrate their fiftieth wedding anniversary; however, when time for the trip came, Matt's delayed retirement caught up with him. They discussed postponing because Matt's knees couldn't take sitting on a plane that long. When they explained the situation to me, I suggested they upgrade their tickets to first-class.

Matt shook his head, "I can't afford first class seats . . ."

I interrupted, "I know you think you can't, Matt. You still think you need to save for retirement, but your retirement is now! That's why I'm giving you permission. In fact, I'm encouraging you to spend your money and enjoy seeing the world with your wife."

I could tell he hated the idea of spending extra money on plane tickets. Matt had developed a strong mindset of saving and refusing to spend. The thought of spending more to be comfortable was something he had never allowed himself to do. Because Matt had worked an additional seven years, he had increased his riches by nearly a million dollars. The cost for them to upgrade so they could take their dream vacation wouldn't begin to touch that sum. Matt and his wife simply needed permission to use the money he'd worked so hard to save to provide enjoyment.

Later, Matt called to tell me he had decided not to purchase those first-class tickets. I was disappointed but took comfort knowing I had done my best to help him live his most contented life.

"It's your money, Matt. You don't have to explain your decisions."

He began to chuckle, "I decided we should go business class."

I joined him in his laughter, and they took their trip.

After their trip, at our next meeting, I asked about their vacation. Matt proceeded to gush like a kid in a candy store, telling me about the in-flight cocktails, the way his chair reclined all the way back, and the hot towel presses the flight attendants gave them. Matt finally started to see all the experiences he'd been missing out on. If only he had listened when I tried to give him permission ten years earlier.

Saving our clients from themselves is one of the most crucial aspects to the job of a financial advisor. When we rethink our job description, we can add abundance, joy and contentment to our client's lives. Advisors work in the permission business. We have the extreme privilege of giving our clients permission to be good stewards of their wealth instead of saving every penny to become rich. This allows them to spend what they have responsibly without a scarcity mentality. As advisors, the more we work to help our clients chase their dreams and find true wealth, the more we develop the Total Relationship mindset.

A change in mindset is the beginning of forming this vital partnership. When we learn to ask the right questions, focus on people rather than products, and give our clients permission to live, we'll be able to protect our clients from themselves. The transition from being a typical money manager into a Total Relationship Advisor begins as we embrace these simple principles.

1. Total Relationship Advisors remember that clients have stories and dreams. Where have they come from? What do they want to do with their money? What's on their bucket list? What things will bring their lives more meaning, not simply more money?

2. Total Relationship Advisors understand the difference between rich and wealthy. We want our clients to find fulfillment and contentment—people who appreciate their past, recognize their accomplishments and blessings, and aren't afraid to live out their dreams.

3. Total Relationship Advisors are in the permission business. Life is short. We want our clients to be prepared for the future, but we don't want them to miss out on the present to do it. We want to find joy in telling our clients what they can do and helping them live the life they can afford to. Allowing our clients to live below their means for no real reason is a disservice to both the clients and ourselves.

CHAPTER SIX:

FOUR PILLARS TO FORM A STRONG PARTNERSHIP

The primary mold that needs to be broken is the focus being solely placed on the money. Too many advisors are stuck in this mold and not allowing enough focus on what the money is for. After we've broken the molds of traditional investing and begun to change the way we view clients, we can build a relationship that will form the foundation needed for a better life.

Early in my career, I read a book by Duncan McPherson which helped shape my investment approach. Though we put a different spin on it, it was McPherson that introduced me to the concept of discovering what clients wanted to use their money for. The Total Relationship is built on four pillars Duncan McPherson called FORM—family, occupation, recreation, and mission.

When advisors focus on these priorities and make them the primary consideration as they invest in clients' lives, they can develop partnerships that will last for years.

YOUR CLIENT'S FAMILY

Many clients make family the central consideration when planning for their future. In my own planning, making certain my children have opportunities for college, and my wife and I can enjoy our senior years top my goal list. The first letter in our acronym teaches advisors to ask clients about their Families first and foremost. The term family generally encompasses one of three groups: children, spouse, or parents. Typically, married couples share long-term goals. And most clients want to set up their children for the greatest chance for success. Sometimes that means buying them a car or paying for college, and other clients want to be able to help financially when grandchildren come. While not everyone has children, everyone has parents, and for many, parents need to be a part of the advisor-client discussion.

A significant percentage of Americans choose to help their aging parents financially. However, many haven't planned for it especially if the need arises suddenly and unexpectedly. Without a plan in place, this kind of significant expense can derail our client's retirement plans. Advisors need to start this critical conversation early no matter how uncomfortable it may be.

According to a recent survey completed by the American Advisors Group (AAG), fifty-five percent of all adult children said they are not financially ready to help their parents when living expenses increase and inflation raises costs more than expected. Over one-third of adult children worry that, over time, their parents will become financial burdens, though nearly half admit they never bring up the subject of finances with their senior parents. [7]

Total Relationship Advisors ask clients about their parents during each annual review to help paint a clear picture of what they may need in the coming years. What we find during this meeting is that many adult children are oblivious to their parents' financial situation. In an attempt to mind their own business, they know nothing about potential debts, loan issues, and more. This can cause serious financial ramifications as retirement draws closer or their parents require end-of-life care. Families cannot plan responsibly for the future if they don't have all the pertinent information. Many clients don't even think to ask their parents these questions until an advisor specifically asks about it. That's why these initial conversations are so crucial to the long-term well-being of the client.

Another study found that nearly half of all respondents admitted that they would rather discuss funeral arrangements with their parents than financial planning.[8] And just over thirty percent said they would be okay inheriting less money if it meant not discussing finances with their parents. These statistics exhibit the extreme reluctance of adult children to initiate uncomfortable conversations with their parents. It is unrealistic for Total Relationship Advisors to expect these adult children to take the initiative when the subject is so obviously a difficult path to traverse. Furthermore, while one-third of GenXers and millennials support their parents financially, already two in five have spent more than $10,000 on their aging parents. [9]

Advisors often omit these sensitive questions assuming the clients' parents have savings to fall back on during their retirement. Despite the common belief that the baby boomer generation has savings for their golden years, almost eighty percent of middle-income sixty- to eighty-year-olds have no savings designated to cover their retirement care. [10]

In the past twenty-five years, I have seen countless clients face financial hardship because one or both of their parents experienced a decline in their health or well-being and had virtually no plan in place for their own care. I have made the mistake of not asking clients specifically about their financial relationships with their parents, and I've seen the massive upheavals that occur when clients have to scramble to support their parents or care for them in their own home. Because family is so important, these unexpected mishaps result in significant commitments of money, time, and other resources. Total Relationship Advisors feel obligated to help clients avoid these all-too-common financial crises.

One of the most unpleasant aspects of this conversation is that people use their parents' lifespan to determine their own. My questions begin with their parent's names, ages, and where they live. I follow up by asking the client how long he or she expects to live. This is a critical factor in creating a life plan. Hereditary health issues could very easily affect our own longevity.

Let's say, for example, I'm speaking to a client in her fifties looking to retire in her sixties. Generally, we would develop a financial plan to ensure she has enough money to last thirty-five years, or to age ninety-five. However, if she adds that both of her parents had health issues that took them in their early sixties, I realize that it will be difficult for her to imagine making it to the edge of a century, and depending on her own health status or how she feels about her parents' health issues, our plan may need to be adjusted.

I've seen clients suddenly thrown into the position of primary trustee or personal representative for their parents' care. This responsibility can cause a lot of turmoil if no one broached the subject before. When the Total Relationship Advisor asks the right questions at the beginning of the relationship, these kinds of upheavals can be avoided. Our onboarding process pushes clients to have tough conversations with their parents. It even allows them to make us the bad guys, "Mom and Dad, I really hate to bother you with this, but my financial advisor says he has to know a few things before he can help me with my investments." It makes me feel good to know I can be the catalyst in initiating important family discussions, saving everyone heartache years down the road.

With family in particular, circling back for updates is essential, not only in developing Total Relationships but also maintaining them. Family ties and health needs change continually, so we need to ask these questions at least annually to allow us to keep our client's portfolio up-to-date and ready to serve them effectively in the future.

Our efforts have the potential to keep our clients out of stressful situations. Clients should not have legal documents rushed to the hospital for signatures because life happened and their plan needs adjusting. It's even more frustrating when these last-minute changes could have been taken care of earlier with proper communication. When Total Relationship Advisors plan ahead and maintain solid communication, we can often keep our clients out of painful positions that demand heavy emotional and financial responses.

An onboarding experience that makes room for open and honest discussion offers clients a chance to get ahead of their future rather than wait for it to come to them. FORM wealth creation begins with Family, and advisors who want the Total Relationship will make this the first point of discussion in every new client relationship.

YOUR CLIENT'S OCCUPATION

The second set of questions a Total Relationship Advisor focuses on relates to the client's Occupation. Simply asking, "What can you tell me about your career?" opens countless doors into your client's life. Having a solid understanding of their occupation is essential to building a successful life plan. While none of us can choose our family or the dynamics that shape it, most have had some say in our occupation. The careers our clients have chosen offer windows into their futures as well as their pasts. Knowing their career choices helps paint a bigger picture of how our clients arrived at their presents. The questions we ask pertaining to occupation give us clues into choices they've made over the years. All these factors play into what they'll need for retirement—something we, at FORM, like to call the last and potentially longest career they will have.

Retirement comes in a variety of flavors. Some clients love what they do. A few found careers they were incredibly passionate about at a youthful age; early networking and experience landed them their dream job. Others found their perfect occupation a bit later in life. The clients in either of those scenarios will likely continue working in their career in some capacity after retirement. Companies are always looking for consultants, part-time employees who will fill in or pick up the slack, and experienced volunteers.

On the other hand, you'll also find clients who have worked with the sole purpose of making a good living and preparing for a carefree future. They may feel indifferent or actively dislike their job, and they wouldn't call it a career. If this group decides to work post-retirement, they'll likely choose a job they've never tried before or move into a field they always wished they'd had the courage to work in.

Regardless of how a client feels about their current occupation, it is important to ask deep, meaningful questions about what kind of dreams they have for their final occupation of retirement and how they would like to live it out.

Many mistakenly believe that a person's annual salary reveals the true value of an occupation. The Total Relationship plan recognizes that a significant career can be measured by the amount of energy and joy it gives. A highly meaningful occupation is determined by so much more than the zeros on the paycheck. Clients base much of their identity on their career choices, but we believe crafting the Total Relationship involves taking a step back and evaluating the contentment and peace of mind a career brings to the life plan.

Part of understanding how the client's occupation will play into their future life plan is hearing the story of their journey. As you listen to the sacrifices, choices, and experiences that brought them to this point, you will learn so much about them.

One of my favorite questions to ask is "What did you want to do when you were a kid?" I believe that all are children at heart, and by probing into their childhood aspirations, we can easily see career possibilities that might excite them or help them unlock dreams they still long to see come true.

Total Relationship Advisors offer clients guidance, and in the occupation department we have an opportunity to contribute greatly. I have helped tons of clients let go of bigger paychecks and jobs that provide comfort but no happiness by simply giving them permission to pursue a career they always wanted but, for assorted reasons, felt they couldn't. Many of my clients have found their quality of life has been enhanced by changing jobs. Some have settled for less money or less convenience. A few have even taken a huge leap of faith.

Sometimes we find people feel trapped in their career. Part of the permission granting business is speaking the difficult truth. Some clients need someone to tell them that they seem unhappy in their current occupation. Others may need us to shed light honestly on their situation to give them the freedom to step into a new venture that will bring more satisfaction.

Many times, I have advised clients to consider trying something different and fun as they prepared for retirement. This is especially helpful if the client does not enjoy his or her current career, has been laid off, or doesn't want to retire fully. I often recommend, "Try it, if you don't like it, quit!" By the time people hit their late fifties or early sixties, it's not about resume building.

My favorite early retirement story features a multimillion-dollar client who took a job as a golf cart attendant. He didn't need the money and would have worked for free if he hadn't wanted to keep his financial status under wraps.

Another client retired at 55 and needed a reason to get out of bed every morning. We discussed options, and he chose a job for the county that started at 5:00 a.m. He spent his days watering the plants on the main streets of his hometown—simple work but enough to motivate him to get up early and enjoy his day.

By treating retirement as a sort of occupation, we can help clients avoid the sense of confusion, boredom, and depression that can come with stepping away from an occupation which for many is a sense of identity.

The occupation conversation continues with finding out what the retirement portion of the client's career will look like. By treating retirement as a sort of occupation, we can help clients avoid the sense of confusion, boredom, and depression that can come with stepping away from an occupation which for many is a sense of identity.

I've found that around eighty percent of retirement transitions are due to outside factors and not necessarily the choice of the employee. Health crises, layoffs, age related triggers, and downsizing often push clients into retirement. Acting preemptively for that day can be beneficial for reducing the side effects of that loss.

George gives us a fitting example. George worked for a medical device company as an engineer analyst. He was a brilliant man and so incredibly detailed I felt a bit nervous to take him on as a client. Frankly, I thought he might drive me nuts. George's analytical persona had spreadsheets for everything retirement related. He and his wife dreamed of selling their home and retiring in the Carolinas.

Very conservative with his spending, George had spent little and amassed much. After we'd met a few times, I explained to George that he could retire much earlier than he had planned. Even though George understood this, his company continued to give him projects and he continued to ask for them—not because he had to, but because he wanted to. George found a deep sense of purpose in his occupation, so leaving it didn't seem like a logical option at that moment. Thus, retirement for George looked a lot like planning to change careers, rather than a time of life.

Every time I talked with George about what he wanted to do, he repeated his longing to move to the South. We finally discussed the possibility of finding the best of both worlds—retiring and taking a part-time job in the area where he wanted to live. George ultimately found a part-time consulting job in South Carolina that allowed him to move into his dream home and use his analytical skills in a whole new way.

Many advisors don't consider themselves career counselors, but occasionally the Total Relationship Advisor sees possibilities that can enhance their client's life—things the client never imagined. Clients need guidance in each phase of their career including the transition into retirement. Attitudes and preparation for that time of life vary from extremely difficult to tremendously exciting. Keeping the client's occupation choices at the forefront of our discussions proves vital as we create the Total Relationship and help our clients sort out what truly matters to them.

YOUR CLIENT'S RECREATION

Creating discussions around Recreation is somewhat unique to the Total Relationship Advisor. Recreation includes hobbies and leisure activities—anything a client participates in for fun. Recreational activities allow clients to focus exclusively on themselves and give them an opportunity to spend time doing something they enjoy.

Learning what our clients love to spend their free time doing is a fast and easy way to get to know them. Furthermore, knowing what they enjoy doing in their leisure can inspire us to support that person in what they love to do. These interests make each Total Relationship exciting and new, because no two clients will ever have the exact same interests and hobbies.

To add to that excitement, recreation passions evolve and change with age, and as we learn new things or become bored with old hobbies, I would venture to say that recreation interests shift every three to five years either marginally or drastically depending on the person. So, just as we do with family and occupation, it is important that we continue to ask what our clients like to do for fun. Understanding a client's likes and dislikes invites fantastic communication and a deeper understanding of who they are.

Leisure activities are deeply important during a person's working years but even more so after they finish a demanding career. Life takes a huge shift when a client moves into the retirement stage. In fact, the change can make for rocky ground for many people. Some clients feel as though they don't know what to do with themselves.

Recreational activities help keep retirees out of that territory of depression and frustration. I've found that helping clients pursue something they love after retirement is incredibly rewarding.

One couple I worked with, Jackson and Leah, embodied this struggle of finding something to fill the time after retirement. Jackson was a partner at a large accounting firm and had a large portfolio. Their goal was to build wealth to cover family expenses and have enough to enjoy life after they retire.

After listening to them tell me about their lives, I asked what they wanted to do during their retirement years. Though retirement wasn't that far off, they seemed unsure; neither wanted to spend every moment with their family, nor did they want to continue working. I asked them what they like to do for fun and what goals they had for their future. Like many successful professionals, their careers and ever-increasing responsibility didn't allow time for much recreation, much less fun. As the career winds down, it is important to rethink activities one can try and enjoy. For Jackson and Leah, I suggested they might have hobbies we could plan for.

One of my favorite things about being a Total Relationship Advisor is becoming an advocate for what our clients love to do. Seeing someone truly passionate about a project, experience, or hobby is awe-inspiring, and financial advisors are in a unique position to help foster the love and joy that comes from recreation. The Total Relationship Advisor cares enough to help clients find purpose beyond work or more money.

Though Leah and Jackson didn't have any specific plans, they knew two things: they wanted to travel, and they loved to golf. After tossing around several ideas wrapped around travel and golfing, we ultimately landed on a goal to play golf in all fifty states. They would be able to enjoy their favorite recreational activity as well as fulfill their longing to travel. Now they had something to look forward to when the time came for them to adjust to their new life position.

I love golf and was thrilled to be a part of helping Leah and Jackson achieve this goal. At each of our annual meetings, I would ask for an update. They told me which states they had been to that year, what they liked about the state and the golf course, and where they would be heading next. After a few years, they had visited every state except Louisiana, Maine, Oregon, and South Carolina. They had enjoyed the journey so much that the idea of completing the goal did not seem to excite them.

Jackson and Leah teach us one more lesson about the discussion of recreational activities and goals with our clients. As they neared the completion of their goal, the idea of golfing in all fifty states had become something of a burden and wasn't as much fun as they initially thought it would be. The beauty of recreational goals is that their entire purpose is to help your clients have fun. Unlike strict financial goals that we need to adhere to in order to achieve our long-term plans, recreational goals are simply meant to be laugh-inducing or peace-bringing activities. So, it's okay to abandon those goals if they no longer add joy to their lives. Crossing off states and traveling was incredibly fulfilling and fun for them in the beginning, but as time went on, they became less motivated to complete it because they didn't have a new goal in place.

During one of our meetings, we recapped their must-haves for their new goal. It needed to be an activity they can do together, something fun they could do with other people, and not physically demanding.

After agreeing to the why behind the what, Jackson asked Leah, "I have always loved the movie *A River Runs Through It*. What about trying Fly Fishing?" Leah agreed. I suggested fishing in the top ten locations in the United States. They both thought that sounded fantastic, and they found someone local to teach them how to fly fish.

What happened next taught me the lesson. Jackson said, "While we are learning to fly fish, let's finish up these few states." Jackson and Leah ultimately decided to finish their original goal once they had a new one to pursue.

As they visit those final states, Jackson and Leah have now taken up fly fishing and are working to win a trophy in the top ten locations in the United States. They love the memories they are creating with these new recreational goals.

The area of recreation creates a phenomenal opportunity for the Total Relationship to develop further than it could ever go if we limited the conversation to finances, family, or occupation. The recreational habits of our clients lets us know them better and more deeply than just numbers in a portfolio. Building true wealth involves learning what our clients love to do and why they love to do it and then crafting goals to offer the greatest level of contentment in their present and their future.

Rather than spending my time talking about the past performance of a portfolio, market, or asset class, I prefer to hear about the size of the fish or what the golf course looks like. Focusing on life and not money, discussing feelings and not only facts, keeps me motivated.

YOUR CLIENT'S MISSION

We complete the Total Relationship FORM by exploring our client's Mission. It's important they have a solid understanding of the impact they want to create, the legacy they want to pass on, and the footprint they want to leave on the lives of those surrounding them.

Mission encompasses the purpose of life; it often drives us and can include family, occupation, and recreational activities. And while we need to plan for these things in the future, I encourage clients to think bigger.

A true mission will give back to the world. It may include family, occupation, and recreation, but each person has the capability to make an impact outside their own bubble. The most difficult part of helping a client discern their mission is opening their eyes to see they can have their fun, help their loved ones, retire well, and still have enough to leave a mark on someone they may never meet.

After the client understands the magnitude of their mission decision, we can begin to look at how the rest of their life complements it. Some will switch career paths or mend a frustrating parental relationship to reach the goal. Others will discover a new hobby—one that offers help to others rather than be a means to self-fulfillment. The beautiful thing about mission is that even though it's meant to be bigger than you, and it's a service to others, it brings tremendous satisfaction. In fact, it's often what wakes you up in the morning and motivates you to keep going when things are hard.

I had a client named Poppy. Poppy loved to give back, whether to charities or the people close to her. She was determined to use her finances to make a difference in the lives of others. When she lost her husband, Poppy kicked her mission mindedness into high gear. She decided to give a large chunk of her Social Security check and pension each month to various people she knew needed it. During every conversation, the kind soul shared how much she loved giving and wished she could do more.

In one of our meetings, I asked what she thought about giving from her portfolio. She had never considered this because she had the extra in her monthly checks. I was surprised she didn't think of it herself; she had a million-dollar-plus portfolio ready to use. I suggested she could use profits from the portfolio in addition to her social security and pension checks.

I asked, "If you could give a significant dollar amount to one place, where would it be?" It didn't take long before she answered, "The church I have attended my entire life is raising money for a building expansion. Do you think I could give some there?" The building project was in the early planning stages, so Poppy was excited that she could make a large, surprise donation to help a place she loved spread more love.

She asked me how much I thought she could give, to which I replied, "Here's my suggestion. It's still early in their building process, so let's draw a line in the sand now. Next year at this time however much your portfolio has grown, we'll donate that net gain to the church." She loved the idea, and we committed to it.

A year later, two things happened. First, thanks to good performance by the market, Poppy's portfolio grew by about $100k. Poppy was elated to give such a large amount to the church. She didn't really want any recognition, though. So, she sent the check anonymously. She told me it was the biggest gift she ever gave. Poppy's church had the seed money they needed to begin the expansion project.

The second thing that happened was the market declined the following year. Much of the profit that was given would have been lost, had she simply held her portfolio. Poppy benefited from having a plan and taking advantage of giving while she was living and when the market provided the extra funds.

Unfortunately, a few years later Poppy was diagnosed with advanced Alzheimer's. Within the next 12 months, I began working with Poppy's distant cousin, Bill. With no kids of her own, Poppy appointed Bill her power of attorney when we did her estate plan years earlier. When it was time to move Poppy into a care facility, Bill asked me to help because Poppy's favorite topic was the $100,000 gift she had given to the church. Poppy had forgotten who Bill was, but when I walked into the room, she looked up with a smile, "Tyson!"

I had advised Poppy for twenty years, so it was my privilege to help Bill take care of her. We settled her into the apartment and put up some of her things. When I left, she seemed not quite at peace, but she was getting used to her new spot in life.

Bill and I drove back to Poppy's house to change out the locks before going to the office to discuss what to do with her property and money. As Bill and I finished swapping the locks, a police siren blared. I finished locking the back door just as the siren stopped. Bill was locking the front door as I came around to the front and saw the cruiser. Confused, I approached the officer, and out from the back seat stepped Poppy screaming and pointing at Bill, "He stole my house!"

The officer explained that Poppy said someone had stolen her house and kicked her out. Bill stood there shocked, trying to explain to the officer what was going on. Poppy was crying and looked at me asking what was going on. We ultimately had to bring out the paperwork and doctor's notes to convince the police officer, and then tried to calm Poppy and attempt to explain her new reality.

She only made it a few more years before passing away. When I attended her funeral, all I could think about was how grateful I was to have played a part in equipping Poppy to fulfill her life's mission. Poppy never saw the building expansion finished, and even if she had, she likely wouldn't have understood what it meant, but I, and everyone at that funeral, knew Poppy had accomplished a mission in her life.

Poppy's story is a phenomenal example of what it looks like to help a client live out their mission, to help them firmly plant the legacy and think bigger than they ever have before. Helping our clients to understand what mission they want to be a part of, especially toward the end of their lives, is a huge part of what a Total Relationship Advisor should be doing.

This wonderful lady ultimately changed the way I view a client's mission as well as the way in which Total Relationship Advisors should be acting within those relationships. Even as Poppy struggled with health issues, it was still my job to make sure her mission was carried out to its fullest extent. It brought me so much joy to see Poppy donate to her church, and I felt just as much heartbreak to see her mind deteriorate so she didn't know it. It reminded me of the importance of helping our clients work towards their legacy at all times because life is so fragile.

Poppy's mission is an example of someone making an outside impact. She constantly focused on giving as much as she could to people she didn't even know at the time.

Many clients focus their mission closer to home. One of my greatest experiences involved the relationship between a father and a son and the mission of the father.

My wife introduced Greg and me. Greg and my wife had known each other in college. We had all become good friends by the time Greg was ready to retire from the pastorate, so he asked my opinion about the best options for his retirement funds.

A very generous man, Greg had very little in the way of savings for retirement. While $100k seemed like a nice sized account to Greg, it's not a lot to last thirty years. As he slowly ate away at his life's bounty, it became clear he was going to run out of savings sooner rather than later. All of this led to the big question: would Greg's father, Charlie, a man in his nineties, leave Greg an inheritance?

Greg's mother, Joan, had been the glue that held the relationship of the father and son together, and after she passed, Charlie and Greg drifted. Charlie had been a very successful businessman and investor, and he didn't really understand Greg's desire to be a pastor. Greg felt he had disappointed his father with his career choice and running out of money would just add to it.

Greg knew his father had built wealth but had no idea how much or what he planned to do with it. Greg was a prime example of someone unable to speak to their parents about finances. On multiple occasions I offered to join him as he had the tough conversation.

Greg had less than a year of savings left when he finally agreed to allow me to talk with his dad. When he finally called his dad to explain he had hired me to help him plan for his future, Greg was pleasantly surprised. His dad was pleased that Greg had an advisor to help him. Plus, he was happy to share his plans with me. So, I drove two and a half hours to meet with Charlie at a country club.

I spent the day with Charlie, listening to his stories and getting to know him better. Charlie pointed out he never used a financial advisor, but he felt better knowing Greg would have one. With great pride, he started telling me his wealth story.

When we finally got to the subject of inheritance, I asked him what he felt his mission was. Charlie understood better than most the idea of wealth stewardship. His deepest desire was to help his family and protect them from themselves.

Charlie knew Greg's generosity had left him with little to no savings, so he wanted to create a plan that would enable him to protect his son, and the rest of the family, from themselves.

Greg's father and I spent the rest of our meeting discussing how best to help his family without entirely rearranging his financial situation. Charlie didn't want to leave everything to Greg, and when I explained that he could also leave funds to his grandchildren using trusts to protect the funds and that he didn't have to wait to die to give to his family, Charlie was thrilled.

He decided on a plan that would give about forty percent to Greg and twenty percent to each of his three grandkids. Since he had lived a good ninety years, he loved that his family could start receiving their inheritance while he was still around to see it. He revealed that he had a nearly seven-million-dollar portfolio that his family had no idea about, and he wanted to be able to continue giving to his family long after he was gone. This was the mission that he cared about, and I had the privilege of helping him implement.

Charlie passed a few years later, during which time we became close as we worked to consolidate his earnings and make arrangements to spread his wealth down his family tree with fairness and generosity. During that time, we talked extensively about Charlie's mission after he was gone. He knew his son and grandkids well, and he knew they wouldn't know what to do with a hefty sum of money. Because of this concern, Charlie had a trust created that would control the funds and see to it that checks were sent as consistently as if Charlie was still around doing it himself.

Those conversations with Charlie set in motion plans that allowed Charlie to provide for Greg and his three children. The interaction also allowed a father and son to reconnect and move past the financial concerns and onto more important matters, like sharing stories of Joan who they both loved and missed.

Charlie died knowing he had protected and preserved his legacy. Because of Charlie's willingness to plan, when Greg's wife struggled with Parkinson's, the trust Charlie created gave them the money to get her the services she needed. I watched Charlie's grandkids pay for their own cars, college, and small vacations as if Charlie was still around giving them money each time they came to visit. It was a privilege to honor Charlie by carrying out his mission long after he was able to see it continue here on Earth.

When we ask our clients about missions they'd like to support, most come down to the people, things, and experiences they care most about. In Poppy's case, she cared about giving generously to people she didn't even know as well as an institution that had given her friendship and spiritual support. Charlie decided to care for his family by protecting them from themselves long after he was gone. Our clients' missions make them special to us and allow us to build the foundation for a Total Relationship. We need to know what wakes them up every morning, what motivates them, and what kind of legacy they dream of leaving during their lifetime. By asking the right questions, we find out about family, occupation, recreation, and mission and can help them live and plan for the best life possible.

SECTION THREE:

A BETTER LIFE SYSTEM

CHAPTER SEVEN:

FORMING A BETTER LIFE FOR YOUR CLIENTS

The Total Relationship Approach invites us to remember one overarching goal: our job is to form a better life for our clients. The phrase "living your best life," though popular in mainstream media, can be difficult to pin down for specific individuals. Though some would like to present a cookie cutter formula to living a great life, the truth is, it's really very ambiguous. Living the "best life" looks incredibly different for everyone. Goals and aspirations will take people in a variety of directions. Fortunately, Total Relationship Advisors know how to ask the right questions. Plus, they have developed a mindset to help craft and mold today's actions into feasible futures.

BETTER LIVES THROUGH THE DETOURS

Clients come to us in various places on the future-planning scale—from those who know exactly what they want from life to those who have little to no idea. Those who can pinpoint their future are ambitious dream-biggers. Occasionally, they fall into the riches-seeking rather than the wealth-stewardship category; regardless, anyone can see this group's connection and commitment to their goals. They carry themselves with certainty, assured of their own success. Though these individuals know what they want, they need an advisor to help them understand how to get there. Total Relationship Advisors assess the clients' goals as well as their current financial status to ensure they are realistic. Then, we help them create life plans that allow them to reach those goals. Some overachievers don't mind working tirelessly to reach ten-, twenty-, and thirty-year milestones. Making every sacrifice the advisor suggests they put into place, these goal-oriented individuals will do whatever it takes to conquer obstacles. Clients on this end of the continuum want a Total Relationship Advisor to help them map out their routes. They won't need their hands held or pushed to succeed.

Clients on the other end of the spectrum come to us with little to no thought about how they would like to spend their retirement. These clients need a different side of the Total Relationship Advisor. They are no less motivated or able to achieve goals, they simply need a bit more direction from their advisors.

Fewer clients have their futures so cleanly planned as the first example, and many fall somewhere in the middle. Those with fewer definitive goals have to first understand their current status. Without that firm foundation, it will be difficult to frame a plan for their future. One of the most important things to remember as we create that road map into the future is that every plan we create, whether the client has their future firmly in their sights or not, will be unique to that client. Portfolios will never be one-size-fits-all because each client has a one-of-a-kind starting point and an exclusive final destination.

Life, like many road trips, affords detours along the way. Things will happen that never could have been anticipated when you mapped out the future. I could share a plethora of instances where I've seen life plans shift and alter routes. These detours aren't limited to tragedies, nor do they only happen to clients.

Life will always be full of twists and turns we don't see coming, and we'll have to adjust our life plans to accommodate the new path.

Total Relationship Advisors understand the fine line between flexibility for life changes and maintaining commitment to the plan. It's a line all clients and advisors walk from time to time throughout their partnership.

BETTER LIVES FOR THOSE WHO ADOPT THE TOTAL RELATIONSHIP MINDSET

The Total Relationship Advisor's primary concern is being a good steward of their clients' wealth. The Total Relationship Advisor uses a system that involves a consistent line of action from the beginning of a new client relationship through his or her end-of-life decisions. We customize each piece so it makes the most sense for each client and allows us to develop a meaningful relationship.

Those who choose to work with financial planners have many options. So, it's important to understand why people might prefer to work with a Total Relationship Advisor over another firm that offers a more traditional philosophy.

Clients choose Total Relationship Advisors because they appreciate the values we bring, the philosophy we follow, and our desire to help make their lives better by focusing on life beyond the money. Deep down, most people understand money means nothing without genuine, lifelong wealth.

We also avoid things that would cause a conflict of interest. For instance, some other firms work under the umbrella of larger companies. This model usually pushes them to recommend the investment products that will bring the biggest benefit to the firm. Total Relationship Advisors are free from sales goals, quotas, and bonus incentives that might inadvertently steer them away from the client's best interest.

Additionally, Total Relationship Advisors understand we can't help everyone. While other firms may compete for the largest number of clients, Total Relationship Advisors aim for the greatest number of life-living clients. We look for clients who agree with our philosophy and want a long-lasting relationship. Our client base focuses on living the best life they can afford. People who seek our services want an advisor who works to know them personally so they can create a comprehensive plan for the future.

Now that we've explored the shift in mindset needed to cultivate a rich Total Relationship, we can look at what a Total Relationship plan will look like in action. The long-lasting design helps clients achieve goals that will outlast them and reach into future generations.

BETTER LIVES WITH THE TOTAL RELATIONSHIP (TR) APPROACH

The Total Relationship Approach has evolved over twenty-five years of experience working with clients. The process involves three steps that address three distinct aspects of the relationship.

TR Planning lays the groundwork for the relationship. It's simply learning as much as possible about the client. Next, we dive into TR Investing. During this step, we focus primarily on learning the financial situation of the client and begin to work together to craft goals that reflect a real and potential future. Finally, TR Care takes us beyond the infant stages of the Total Relationship. Here, we implement the portfolio with the Total Relationship Advisor stepping into the role of coach and teacher.

Each section of the Total Relationship Approach works cohesively with the others and fulfills our company goal of creating the best environment possible for the success of the client. This design has allowed hundreds of Total Relationships to be built and puts all we've learned about what it takes to have one into action.

CHAPTER EIGHT:

TOTAL RELATIONSHIP PLANNING

Total Relationship Planning allows us to form a solid understanding of who the client is and why he or she wants our help. No story is the same. Backgrounds, cultural nuances, education, family diversity, and more affect how clients view the world, the way they handle their money, and the goals they decide to set.

It is essential to remember that new clients will expect a conversation about returns, markets, dividends, and investments, so when we begin to ask them about themselves, they may be taken aback.

In addition to getting to know clients during our first meeting, we want them to understand that no matter what they have or are working toward, money itself is not our main objective. In the Total Relationship, money is the means to a better life. Money works as uniquely within each portfolio as the individual and their loved ones. By the time clients finish this initial conversation, they should clearly understand our interest in who they are as people. Each person is more than a client, investor, or dollar amount.

In order to create the Total Relationship plan, discovery is vital. Discovery boils down to asking the right questions. In his book *The Dan Sullivan Question*, Dan challenges us. "If we were having this discussion three years from today, and you were looking back over those three years, what has to have happened in your life, both personally and professionally, for you to feel happy with your progress? Specifically, what dangers do you have now that need to be eliminated, what opportunities need to be captured, and what strengths need to be maximized?" It's that kind of approach we take with the Total Relationship. Though it might seem foreign to them at first, your clients will love talking about their kids, their hopes, and their next planned vacation. When clients know we care about their personal and professional future and realize we want to help them use their finances to reach their goals, we open a space where they feel comfortable sharing their hearts and their lives.

We begin by identifying the amount of money that should not be invested in addition to traditional planning. While this seems counter-intuitive to some, we seek to set aside six to twenty-four months of regular cash flow to accommodate a client's needs in case of emergency. Then we dig deeper with the Total Relationship *Discovery Deck.*

These cards have questions that invite the client to share things that will allow us to move forward in their best interest. When the client feels as though we care, they will grow comfortable reaching out with questions and additional pertinent information. This part of the process sets the foundation for a relationship that has longevity and commitment. The unique answers we receive to these questions will give us a blueprint for the best way to proceed as we build lasting wealth for people who trust us.

ESTATE & LEGACY PLANNING CARD

For many, leaving a legacy is a primary focus of their long-term financial goals. Though the thought of death can make for a difficult subject, everyone, even those who don't want to talk about passing, want to make sure their assets end up where they want them after they're gone. This means Total Relationship Advisors ignore the hesitation, reluctance, and stress and face the necessity of having the hard conversation. Let's face it, it will be easier for clients to talk to an advisor than their families, so it's up to us to ensure they make their wishes known so they can be honored after they're gone or if a time comes when they can't speak for themselves. Our *Discovery Deck* questions offer an outlet for this uncomfortable topic by focusing on the positivity accumulated wealth can bring.

These questions help clients fulfill their mission even after they're gone. Some, like Charlie, want to take care of their loved ones as long as possible, perhaps for generations after they've gone. Others, like Poppy, who don't have a family or are blessed with loved ones who have garnered their own success, put their emphasis on helping those they never met. Asking clients about charities and foundations offers them a chance to make a lasting difference. Trusts and endowments can live for decades or centuries beyond the ones who create them.

In order to best assist clients in fulfilling their mission beyond this life, the Total Relationship *Discovery Deck* asks these questions:

1. How much money would you like to leave your loved ones?
2. What legacy do you want to leave after you have taken care of those you love?
3. Which organization or causes do you support or wish to support in the future?

CARING FOR PARENTS AND/OR ADULT CHILDREN CARD

The next section of our *Discovery Deck* continues in the vein of family and loved ones. Family brings joy to the lives of many people. Though often a source of unpredictability, many of the unknowns of family life can be included in our preparations.

In addition to weddings, cars, and college—all things that allow us to have some control of the costs—discussing care for aging parents and disabled adult children is a necessity. As I mentioned, few people have sit-down conversations with their parents about their wishes as they age. *Discovery Deck* questions help initiate that conversation. The Total Relationship Advisor's willingness to listen and engage in this difficult conversation is an essential part of the job.

Along the same lines as that discussion, the family with adult children unable to care for themselves must prepare. Parents who know they will outlive a disabled or severely limited child sometimes lie awake at night worrying about the future of their loved one. If we know the needs at the beginning of the Total Relationship, we can alleviate that worry by showing the client how their precious one will be cared for long after they're gone. Family, even with all the dynamics that make it difficult, will almost always be the most important aspect of your clients' lives. When clients see us treat this part of their future with the care and attention it deserves, the relationship will quickly move from advisor to friend.

Building trust with clients in the initial interview will be even easier when they know we care more about the future of their families than we do their bank accounts. These family related *Discovery Deck* questions help move us in that direction:

1. How do you see your current family situation changing over the next ten to twenty years?
2. Do you expect to care for your parents and/or adult children?
3. What conversations have you had with your parents and/or adult children on this subject?

PLANNING TO MAKE SURE YOU DON'T OUTLIVE YOUR ASSETS CARD

No one wants to face their mortality, and asking someone to guesstimate how long they will live can feel wrong. Regardless, the uncomfortable subject is necessary. Being unprepared for financial crises twenty or thirty years down the road will always be worse than talking about it now.

Approaching the topic of predicted lifespan becomes a little easier with the *Discovery Deck*. When the questions are part of a pre-planned list, it sets the client at ease.

Treating this delicate subject with respect helps build trust and comfort between an advisor and a client. Fortunately, we can piggyback this conversation with the estate and legacy portion. It will be encouraging for clients to know that if they prepare for the worst, and it doesn't happen, they'll have a nice nest egg to share with their loved ones. The longevity questions we ask, look something like this:

1. Does longevity run in your family?
2. Do you think you will outlive your assets, or will your assets outlive you?
3. Do your projections include living until age 80, 90, or even 100?

TRAVEL & LEISURE PLANS CARD

We already discussed the importance of knowing your clients' recreational dreams. Unfortunately, many advisors forget or don't see the need to ask about leisure activities and passion projects, but Total Relationship Advisors make it a priority. Travel can be one of the most costly leisure expenses, especially in retirement. When couples finally have free time, seeing the sites seems like a reward for all their hard work. A ski trip in the Alps or a cruise in the Mediterranean can cause a huge hole in the portfolio if we don't prepare.

Not only that, the hours gained when they give up the nine-to-five opens up time for hobbies. Car enthusiasts, for example, could have a major surprise retirement expense if the advisor glosses over the right questions. Asking clients about their hobbies and activities offers a glimpse into our clients' passions and core beliefs. Paying attention to these interests gives advisors a window into their clients' lives.

I personally like to talk about the client's bucket list. This list of dream experiences helps Total Relationship Advisors know how to plan so they can give clients permission to live their absolute best lives. One of the most rewarding parts of being a Total Relationship Advisor lies in the permission business we've talked about. It's fun watching clients' faces when they realize they can check things off that dream list, especially if they always assumed it would be financially impossible. Bucket list items can be as small as achieving a specific position at work to as large as spending a few months in Bali, but deciding what is achievable and making it happen is a core focus for Total Relationship Advisors.

The *Discovery Deck* questions that help us plan for exciting recreation and leisure include these:

1. How much do you plan to travel when you have the time?
2. What leisure activities or hobbies do you enjoy or look forward to trying?
3. What is on your "bucket list"?

RETIREMENT PLANNING CARD

One of the most common reasons people invest is so they know they can enjoy their retirement. Others come to financial advisors looking for ways to enjoy their life now while they make certain they have enough to enjoy life in retirement too.

Every person imagines retirement a bit differently. Some envision vacations, others volunteering, and a few just want to spend time with loved ones. Total Relationship Advisors never assume retirement will look the same for every client.

With the variety of options Social Security and pension accounts give to retirees, the subject of age will be dramatically different for each client. The longer we wait for retirement, the more money we can get from Social Security because we'll obviously have less time to use it. Some pension plans offer similar variables, and 401ks and IRAs have regulations all their own. So, each client's timeline for retirement and the feasibility for that age will vary greatly. Additionally, the amount the client will need during retirement will depend on how they want to spend those years and the way of life they've grown accustomed to. Because of these variables, the amount of money each client will need will differ.

Some clients will prefer an early retirement, whereas others may want to work as long as they can, whether it be for the love of the job or the identity their career brings. Other clients may work longer to save money for future generations, while another group might decide to work longer to net a larger annual income during retirement.

Three simple questions help us map out our client's journey to financial freedom during retirement:

1. What do you want your future retirement to include?
2. At what age do you want to stop working, and do you plan to work in retirement?
3. What annual income will you need to maintain your current standard of living?

BUSINESS TRANSITION & SUCCESSION CARD

We have a few questions specifically geared toward entrepreneurs. Entrepreneurs are typically driven and dedicated to their career choices. Most of these business owners started small. Some worked as solopreneurs out of their basement or garage until their business grew. Their business will feel like their baby. Commitments within their companies and the love they have for this entity they created consumes their time. Asking the right questions can help Total Relationship Advisors gauge the role the client's occupation plays in his or her life. Entrepreneurs often don't take time to think about the way their retirement will impact the company. By presenting the scenario early in the relationship, advisors can save their clients a lot of time and potential problems down the road when they inevitably do step down.

In particular, asking what happens if they can't go into work tomorrow forces them to put contingency plans in place for unpredictable things like accidents and health problems. Plan B allows a buffer for financial planning and gives advisors a chance to get ahead of any unforeseeable circumstances.

At FORM Wealth, we ask entrepreneurs three unique questions:

1. How do you see your business evolving?
2. Do you have a transition/succession process or plan in place? Have you discussed it with those who will be most affected?
3. What happens if you can't go to work tomorrow?

EDUCATION PLANNING CARD

Education is a fantastic topic to bring up with clients. It has aspects of all four of the FORM pillars. Education impacts each sector of our lives. Some clients will opt for education for themselves so they can better support their family or secure promotions in their occupations. Others will focus on paying for their child's education or providing assistance to their grandchildren, nieces, nephews, or friends—anyone they have a relationship with. They simply want to help improve the lives of those they care about. It might even mean creating a mission by setting up a scholarship fund with their excess.

Learning about the client's past education can help us as we advise and counsel, especially if we discover a different occupation could increase their overall happiness. Even if their education is a trade school or random classes, these answers can help us learn about their passions or interests.

Some of my clients help their children through college because they feel it is a necessity. Others believe supporting their children as they pay their own way through school better helps them learn the value of money. Regardless of your opinion, with the cost of education in the twenty-first century, it is certainly something to be discussed as early as possible.

Total Relationship Advisors ask these questions to help their clients prepare to better themselves or help others with their education:

1. What new skills and knowledge would you like to pursue in the future?
2. Where would you like your children or grandchildren to go to school?
3. To what level would you like to support their education?

Learning the answers to these questions of our *Discovery Deck* paints a picture of our clients' future goals. This knowledge allows Total Relationship Advisors to see which strategies will best help the client. After we understand their plans, we can start asking questions so we better understand which investments will be best for this particular client.

CHAPTER NINE:

TOTAL RELATIONSHIP (TR) INVESTING

The second stage in launching the Total Relationship is TR Investing. In the investing stage, the *Discovery Deck* questions focus on putting what's possible into terms the client can see and understand. As we explore the details of the client's personal and financial circumstances, we help them refine and document their goals, and finally analyze their current and potential courses of action.

Most clients rely on financial advisors simply to be portfolio managers. However, money management is only one service that Total Relationship Advisors provide.

When considering the best way to manage any portfolio, we first examine the collection of answers the client gave in the TR Planning phase. Total Relationship Advisors use an income planning process that dives into the larger picture of the client's priorities. With those goals in mind, the professional suggests the best investments for that client. The planning process helps to clarify and direct all streams of incoming wealth including active, passive, and portfolio income. One-size-fits-all money management solutions are a misnomer. By using an adaptive plan, Total Relationship Advisors are able to create a customized portfolio specific to each client.

This individualized treatment adds to the environment of trust created in the first *Discovery Deck* phase—perhaps the most important element of the Total Relationship—and allows us to maintain clarity throughout the process of getting to know our clients.

PLANNING FOR MARKET DECLINE CARD

Market decline can send some clients into a panic. Others, especially those who have experienced the ups and downs of investing, remain confident and comfortable when things start to look shaky. Listening to their previous investing stories opens a window into their investment decision thought process. We also get a glimpse into how they react and what they've learned from their mistakes. This knowledge helps us understand how our clients will see future investments.

The questions in this part of the *Discovery Deck* assist us in gauging a client's reaction to market conditions.

The final question could be asked in reverse, asking what a client may do if the market increases by 20%. While there is no right or wrong reaction, knowing how the client perceives market fluctuations helps Total Relationship Advisors have a better understanding of how to approach clients with news of market changes. The way we communicate with the client is an important aspect of maintaining strong relationships. These questions give Total Relationship professionals guidance as they make investment recommendations:

1. What is your personal experience with market declines?
2. What was your worst investment, and in what way has it affected how you invest?
3. If your investments dropped 20% tomorrow, what would you do and how would you feel?

RISK MANAGEMENT CARD

Most of us don't like to think about taking risks with our finances. In order to understand a client's overall relationship to money, we have to discern how they feel about risk-taking. Just as with anything, some are far more willing to take risks if it means the possibility of a higher yield. One perspective isn't better than the other, but knowing the client's willingness to take risks builds trust.

Along that same vein, we'll find that one group of clients wants to be involved in every move we make in their portfolio, while a second group thinks ignorance is bliss. For that second group our annual meeting or quarterly statements may be enough.

Either way, it's important to know how often a client wants to hear what is going on in their portfolio and to what extent they want to be involved in the decision making. Recognizing their level of concern will help us to be the best Total Relationship Advisor possible.

In order to ascertain the level of risk our clients are willing to take, we recommend asking the following questions:

1. In life and in investing, are you a risk-taker or a risk-avoider?
2. Do you manage your risk exposure or prefer to delegate risk to an advisor?
3. When it comes to money, what makes it hard for you to sleep at night?

TAXES & INFLATION CARD

Though almost everyone enjoys smooth roads and safe streets, few like to think about taxes. Attitudes range from indifference to genuine hatred, and understanding the individual client's take on the subject is essential to planning portfolios. Many are accustomed to having the taxes deducted before they see their check. When they begin to pull from their investments, this could change. Understanding how your client will perceive that shift makes the advisor's job easier in the years to come.

In addition, Total Relationship Advisors prepare clients for cost-of-living changes. The value of a million dollars drops substantially every decade. Part of our responsibility is educating the client so they can see what their money will look like when they reach retirement age. First, we have to determine their awareness of the effects of inflation on their assets. Creating a plan to offset the rising costs will save grief and financial strain in the future, but until clients understand the need to keep their investments growing faster than the rate of inflation, they may question our recommendations.

To decide how much we need to teach the clients about how inflation will affect their tax liability and their investments, we ask a few questions:

1. How do you think your plans for retirement will change your tax burdens?
2. What are you doing today to minimize your tax liability?
3. What plan do you have to offset the rising costs of your standard of living?

After going through the *Discovery Deck*, advisors have a better understanding of who the clients are as people.

Uncovering a client's underlying values, hopes, and aspirations allows for a better understanding of how to build wealth and develop wealth stewardship in the lives of our clients. After learning about their lives, the TR Planning phase concludes with a Life Plan to help ensure a strong understanding of the client's FORM priorities so we can both have a clear picture of what to expect as we move forward.

TR Planning is the foundational building block of the Total Relationship and allows us to provide the best service when we start TR Investing. As we begin to know clients more intimately in all areas of their lives, our interest in them becomes more genuine, and it shows. When the client sees that we care about the intricacies of their lives, the level of trust required for the Total Relationship rises. From here, Total Relationship Advisors envision the countless possibilities that lie ahead for their clients.

The investing portion of the Total Relationship concludes with an Investment Policy Statement, or an IPS. An IPS provides transparency and clarifies the decision-making parameters as FORM advisors structure the client's portfolio. Clarity within investment plans is important to the client, and it should be important to the ideal Total Relationship professional as well.

We create the Life Plan and review it annually to make certain we have a strong understanding of the client's priorities, and they have a clear picture of what they can expect from their Total Relationship Advisor.

CHAPTER TEN:

TOTAL RELATIONSHIP (TR) CARE

The TR Investment Strategy is a customized process that explains the roles and responsibilities of the Total Relationship Advisor. We transfer assets between investments, cash reserves, and bank accounts based on the specific needs of each client, and we focus on short-term as well as long-term priorities in all areas.

The final step in being a Total Relationship professional involves a consistent effort on the part of the advisor to be ever learning in preparation to help in every area of our clients' lives. This enables the advisor to offer a long-term commitment and wealth stewardship in the form of Total Relationship Care.

TR Care helps clients achieve their plan and fulfill their purpose. Caring goes beyond investing. It is our long-term commitment to the Total Relationship. We ground the client's portfolio recommendations in risk tolerance analysis, time horizon, investment objectives, and income needs. Together these make a strong beginning for the Total Relationship, but the care and serving aspect continues long after.

Total Relationship client care begins with coaching and remaining an advocate throughout the entirety of the relationship. TR Care understands and offers a commitment to work with clients as their lives shift. Total Relationship Advisors want clients to enjoy the journey while preparing for the future. We enable them to enjoy their best lives by giving them permission to live to their fullest potential—financially and emotionally.

TRANSFORMING WEALTH INTO VALUE FOR LIFE

From the time I turned five until I left for college, my grandparents lived right across the street from us. Grandma and Grandpa Ray had a huge, elegant home and a membership at the private Bigfoot Country Club in Fontana-on-Geneva-Lake, Wisconsin. They dined at nice restaurants regularly and had sporty convertibles that were the envy of their neighbors. You might call them the Joneses of their neighborhood. Their lives seemed perfect to those around them, including myself.

Grandma Ray was born in 1919 and came of age during the Great Depression. She married my grandfather at age eighteen, after which he joined the service. After my grandfather served his country, they had kids, and Grandpa Ray took a union job. When he filled out his pension paperwork, he checked the box that would give them the most money when he retired. Unfortunately, it meant the money would only last for his lifetime.

Grandma Ray ended up living for many years alone on the poverty wage of a social security check. Within five years of his death, she had depleted all her extra assets.

When I began my financial services career in 1998, I found out my grandmother was broke. Grandma said to me, "Save your money, kid. Poverty sucks."

Grandpa Ray had spent money like a rich man after he retired. Learning the truth of their financial status shattered my image of them—happy, without a financial care in the world. In hindsight, my Grandpa's biggest mistake wasn't the box he checked on his pension plan. The greater mistake was that he had never created an investment strategy to fund their future.

Grandma Ray passed away at 103 years old after living thirty years in poverty. Her story taught me that planning for the future is an absolute necessity to becoming successful in the pursuit of true wealth. Decisions made today directly impact the future. The biggest risk to any investment strategy is not planning for the unpredictability of the future. My grandparents' story inspired me to focus on this Total Relationship Approach.

Many people would be set up for a beautiful future and avoid financial upheaval if they simply had a bit of help from someone who understands how the system works. I've built my career around becoming the kind of person who creates Total Relationships. I love offering advice and helping where and when clients need it most. It has been so rewarding to see the work I've put into these relationships make meaningful change in the lives of my clients.

Knowing I can help people like my Grandma Ray has encouraged me to forge ahead on my journey of helping clients build true wealth within their financial and personal lives, and I think about her every time I help a client avoid late-life poverty and watch them live their dream life.

CHAPTER ELEVEN:

ADOPTING THE MINDSET OF A TR ADVISOR

When advisors adopt the principles of the Total Relationship, they find that each conversation develops into a unique journey. It's a lot like using a compass. True North stays the same, much like our core values; however, each person will offer a new perspective and a one-of-a-kind road to follow. Each turn will add color and beauty to our lives, and if we're doing it right, it will add abundance to our clients' lives, too.

Hopefully, since you've made it this far, the concept of the Total Relationship Advisor has resonated with you. If you're a client, you can adopt this mindset as you look for a financial advisor willing to ask the tough questions and come alongside you as you live life well.

Financial advisors who adopt this philosophy become men and women who help clients build wealth and achieve long term goals through consistency and patience. They understand that traditional molds of financial advising have become outdated, and they bring innovative ideas to the table. You can adopt these Total Relationship principles to create a better experience for clients. Focusing on profit rather than people makes it impossible to cultivate this novel approach.

If you're part of a team that still focuses on portfolio management, marketing, running the business, recruiting, and prospecting, embracing the Total Relationship mindset may mean breaking away from your current firm. That kind of team probably won't provide the flexibility of moving from uniform advising into informed advising. You may never be able to convince them to abandon the cookie cutter ideas that mimic the approach everyone has been using since the dawn of financial advising. The company that uses yesterday's lottery numbers and focuses on bigger assets and better production misses the most crucial factor in financial advising—client connection.

Adopting the Total Relationship strategy will be easier for the advisor who owns his or her own firm or joins a firm that already has this approach. You'll have the latitude to build those personal relationships with each and every client. You can become their coach and make a real difference in the lives of your clients.

The Total Relationship means celebrating accomplishments and extraordinary moments as well as having the difficult conversations necessary to earn the client's trust. Total Relationship Advisors review their clients' lives on a regular basis, and if they work with a Total Relationship team, everyone on the team cares about what happens in their lives.

When you adopt this mindset, you begin to understand that each client and situation will be different than any before or after. And if you're adopting this mindset on your own, I don't want to leave you without a reminder that appeasement is the road to nowhere. It will be difficult, especially if you're changing strategies on some of your long-term investors, but you have to be willing to push back when the client wants to make poor financial decisions. Regardless of how upset they become when it seems like you won't listen, they will be grateful later when they see the payoff of your persistence.

If you have an entire team working with you, it's much easier to adopt the Total Relationship mindset. I'm blessed to have a full staff who all embrace this idea of knowing our clients so well we can nearly predict what they'll want to do next with their funds. Everyone, including our support staff, understands the crucial need to ask the right questions and pay attention to changes in our clients' lives.

I can't tell you that adopting this mindset and making the necessary changes will be easy, but I can tell you it will be worth it. You'll feel better about yourself as you become a vital part of your clients' future. If you're an advisor that loves the idea of a great client-advisor relationship, the Total Relationship Approach gives you the framework to have the conversation that will allow you to go deeper.

If you'd like to journey further than merely adopting this mindset, I have good news. After twenty-five years of refining these practices, we have developed some systems that help us build relationships and alleviate some of the burden in the office, and we love to share them with like-minded advisors.

ALIGN YOURSELF WITH IDEAL OF THE TOTAL RELATIONSHIP

People tell me I'm a great storyteller; however, that's only because my experiences with clients have taught me tremendous lessons, some from a more tragic perspective than others. It's those tragedies that make me even more passionate about helping clients live their best life. And the blessing I feel when I can help these new friends drives me to invite advisors to align with me and break those old molds of money management.

My clients are more than their money. Their missions, goals, and achievements compel me to do what I do. The deep relationships I've built set me on the road to creating the Total Relationship Approach so other financial advisors can learn from my mistakes as well as my successes. Every interaction convinces me that this career offers more potential than I had originally thought possible.

To free up time to focus on the relationships, we've had to find a solution to automate the investments and the running of the business. On my own, I'd never have the resources to engage in the number of conversations needed to make a living and still do what's best for the clients. So, we have built a team and developed systems to make the process run more smoothly.

We've created guides that help the advisors on our team move the answers from our *Discovery Deck* to practical applications, and we've developed software to track our clients lives. Plus, as we find additional ways to make it easier to spend time on the relationship and put our best practices in place for clients, we incorporate them into our system.

For advisors who want to take a step beyond adopting the principles and strategies we've discussed, my team has created space at TotalRelationship.com to offer tools that will allow advisors to align themselves with the Total Relationship Approach and give them access to every resource and automation we use as well as those that will be developed in the future.

ACCOMPANY ME AS I CONTINUE LIVING OUT THE TOTAL RELATIONSHIP

Forming Total Relationships with clients can be challenging work; it requires attention, dedication, and determination. But when we see our clients living their best lives and know it's because we were able to give them the permission and guidance they needed so they could chase their dream or reach that goal, every ounce of effort feels painless. When one of my clients sends his children to college free of student loans or retires five years earlier than anticipated, I celebrate. The hours I put in pay off when clients call with heartfelt thanks for helping them through some of the most grim times in their lives. Plus, I get to support them and be their cheerleader during the fun times. I can feel good about myself, knowing that, in the end, I made a lasting impact because of the energy I put into the Total Relationship.

I've been asked why people choose a Total Relationship Advisor over other financial advisors. First, our clients appreciate the Total Relationship philosophy and values.

It's important to them that we want to make their lives better, rather than just bring them more money. A lot of them come to us after spending years of having no say in how their money was invested because an employer decided where the 401K was held or their advisor just focused on the investments. Finding someone who will listen to their plans and devote time and energy into getting to know them gives them confidence in their future.

Most of our clients also value the fact we have no product to offer them. There is no fund or proprietary investment strategy. We avoid the conflict of interest that can exist when a person works for a financial services company. At the end of the day, the advisor who works for one of those big companies is beholden to their employer. A lot of those big box companies let anyone open an account and give them money.

Total Relationship Advisors seek clients that fit. We aren't a one-stop-shop for everyone. We look for people who want a holistic financial plan and want a relationship that will last for decades. While other firms often send clients through a rotation of advisors depending on who answers the phone, Total Relationship Advisors cherish their clients and know their history; we want to sit down and have a conversation that will take into consideration the client's complete financial situation.

I invite all financial advisors to consider this Total Relationship Approach. It doesn't matter what career stage you are in; you can align your vision with this concept and adopt the approach.

Going it alone in this industry can be tough. Even if you're aligned with our values and have adopted the Total Relationship mindset, you might need more. I enjoy meeting with others in the industry to share my vision and partner with them in the Total Relationship. Even geography can't stand in the way of us journeying together to change the world of financial advising one client connection at a time.

Changing our mindset can be difficult, but adapting and evolving as we learn more about the ways clients want to be seen and heard is one of the most important things we can do as advisors. Building Total Relationships will break those old molds and cultivate new models that better serve our clients and our community. I welcome advisors who've embraced the Total Relationship mindset to join my team.

The ancient Greeks used the word paraclete to mean advisor, but the expression has a rich meaning we can apply to the Total Relationship. A paraclete or parakletos was more than just an advisor, he was able to offer consolation as well as be an advocate and an intercessor. The paraclete took on the roles of helper, comforter, and counselor. The Total Relationship Advisor does more than just sit in an office and keep an eye on funds, he acts as his clients' paraclete.

When advisors embrace their role as coach, comforter, teacher, advocate, intercessor, counselor, and friend, their ability to make a difference increases exponentially. Total Relationship Advisors come alongside their clients aligning with their values and deepest desires to help steer them toward the most abundant life possible.

Accompanying those working toward the Total Relationship is one of my greatest passions; that's why you'll see joy when I share my stories at every speaking engagement and hear me elaborate during my podcasts. It's also why I created a firm that allows likeminded advisors to come together and break the mold of this industry. Rather than forging ahead alone in this industry, we can come together to be part of the great energy that is created when like-minded individuals partner to make a powerful impact in the lives of people all over this wonderful planet. Join me in the Total Relationship approach as we break molds, transform relationships, and build true wealth.

ABOUT THE AUTHOR

After graduating from the honors program at the University of West Florida, Tyson Ray spent more than twenty-five years continuing to expand his knowledge and expertise through Yale School of Management, CIMA® Certification Registration Education Program, and the College for Financial Planning. Tyson also received certification in Business Exit Planning to better help entrepreneurs and business owners transition into retirement or a new field by selling their life's work.

Tyson Ray CFP®, CExP®, CIMA® FORM | CEO, Founding Partner and RJFS Senior Wealth Advisor has been named a 2018-2023 Forbes Best-in-State Wealth Advisor, 2021-2023 Barron's Top 1200, and a 2005-2023 Raymond James Chairman's Council Advisor. He is also a member of the Financial Planning Association of Wisconsin. The community has recognized Mr. Ray for his many philanthropic endeavors by granting him the *Invest in Others Global Community Impact Award* among others. Additionally, *Wealth Management* has acknowledged his ongoing work with his non-profit, Children's World Impact, by awarding him the Advisor with a Heart Award for Sustainable Charity.

ENDNOTES

1 Imig, Paul. "The Majority of Americans Say Their Financial Planning Needs Improvement, But Only a Third Seek Professional Help." *Northwestern Mutual.* July 27, 2022 https://news.northwesternmutual.com//2022-07-27-The-Majority-of-Americans-Say-Their-Financial-Planning-Needs-Improvement,-But-Only-a-Third-Seek-Professional-Help.

2 "Hypothetical Outcomes of Crisis Periods." November 4, 2019. https://www.dalbar.com/portals/dalbar/cache/docs/Hypothetical%20Outcomes%20of%20Crisis%20Periods%20v3.pdf

3 Bhaimiya, Sawdah "The number of Americans earning over $100,000 who are living paycheck to paycheck is climbing as inflation squeezes households, survey shows." *Insider.* January 31, 2023. https://www.businessinsider.com/americans-earning-over-100000-living-paycheck-to-paycheck-2023-1.

4 The Investopedia Team. "What is a Recession." *Investopedia.* March 28, 2023. https://www.investopedia.com/terms/r/recession.asp.

5 Chetty, Raj; Friedman, John N.; Stepner, Michael and The Opportunity Insights Team. "The Economic Impacts of COVID-19: Evidence from a New Public Databuse Built Using Private Sector Data. *NBER Working Paper Series.* https://www.nber.org/system/files/working_papers/w27431/w27431.pdf.

6 Viguerie, Patrick; Calder, Ned; Hindo, Brian. "2021 Corporate Longevity Forecast." *Innosight.* May 2021. https://www.innosight.com/insight/creative-destruction/.

7 "Over 50% of Generation X Can't Afford to Help their Senior Parents" *AAG.* August 9, 2022. https://www.aag.com/company-news/press-release/over-50-of-generation-x-cant-afford-to-help-their-senior-parents/

8 Wells Fargo. "Survey: Financial Planning & Preparedness of Americans with Parents Entering Retirement." 2022. https://stories.wf.com/wp-content/uploads/2022/12/Wells-Fargo-Financial-Planning-Survey-Report.pdf.

9 "Caring For Aging Parents: New GoHealth Study Details How Gen Xers and Millennials Are Impacted. *GoHealth.* October 8, 2020. https://www.gohealth.com/new-gohealth-report-reveals-seniors-rely-on-families-for-support-with-healthcare-and-finances/.

10 CSR Researchers. "Retirement Care Realities For Middle-Income Boomers" *Center for a Secure Retirement.* December 16, 2020. https://www.centerforasecureretirement.com/posts/retirement-care-realities-for-middle-income-boomers

Explore the
TOTAL RELATIONSHIP

Download Comprehensive
Client & Advisor Questions at:

FORMwealth.com/book

CONNECT WITH TYSON

FORMwealth.com/book